P9-DFO-871

"Steve Mosley masterfully plants the seeds of God's promises in the heart of the reader in his new book, *Secrets of the Mustard Seed*. The impact will be fully developed as the reader responds to God's love and chooses daily to incorporate these life-changing promises into the daily walk."

— Daniel F. Houghton, president,
Hart Research Center

"Steve Mosley is not only a wordsmith, but he's also an artist with a marvelous blend of theology to create word-pictures through his gift of writing. Steve has blessed millions through his creative pen. I'm happy to place every confidence that *Secrets of the Mustard Seed* will be life-changing for all who embark on a spiritual venture by reading this book."

— E. Lonnie Melashenko, speaker;
director, Voice of Prophecy

"For all of Steven Mosley's illustrious career as a writer of Christian literature, he has bested himself this time. *Secrets of the Mustard Seed* is interesting, inspiring, and useful. The sequence of comparatives and contrasts are food for deep thinking. This book is a must-read for every serious seeker for the real answer."

— Daniel G. Matthews, president, HisKids Incorporated;
speaker/emeritus, Faith for Today Television

Secrets OF THE MUSTARD SEED

TEN LIFE-CHANGING PROMISES FROM THE NEW TESTAMENT

STEVEN MOSLEY

NAVPRESS

Bringing Truth to Life

P.O. Box 35001, Colorado Springs, Colorado 80935

OUR GUARANTEE TO YOU

We believe so strongly in the message of our books that we are making this quality guarantee to you. If for any reason you are disappointed with the content of this book, return the title page to us with your name and address and we will refund to you the list price of the book. To help us serve you better, please briefly describe why you were disappointed. Mail your refund request to: NavPress, P.O. Box 35002, Colorado Springs, CO 80935.

The Navigators is an international Christian organization. Our mission is to reach, disciple, and equip people to know Christ and to make Him known through successive generations. We envision multitudes of diverse people in the United States and every other nation who have a passionate love for Christ, live a lifestyle of sharing Christ's love, and multiply spiritual laborers among those without Christ.

NavPress is the publishing ministry of The Navigators. NavPress publications help believers learn biblical truth and apply what they learn to their lives and ministries. Our mission is to stimulate spiritual formation among our readers.

www.navpress.com
Library of Congress Catalog Card Number: 20002002124
ISBN 1-57683-317-8

Cover design by Ray Moore
Cover photo by Ray Moore
Creative Team: Brad Lewis, Amy Spencer, Pat Miller

Some of the anecdotal illustrations in this book are true to life and are included with the permission of the persons involved. All other illustrations are composites of real situations, and any resemblance to people living or dead is coincidental.

Unless otherwise identified, all Scripture quotations in this publication are taken from the HOLY BIBLE: NEW INTERNATIONAL VERSION® (NIV®). Copyright © 1973, 1978, 1984 by International Bible Society. Used by permission of Zondervan Publishing House. All rights reserved. Other versions include the *New American Standard Bible* (NASB), © The Lockman Foundation 1960, 1962, 1963, 1968, 1971, 1972, 1973, 1975, 1977; the *Amplified New Testament* (AMP), © The Lockman Foundation 1954, 1958; and the *King James Version* (KJV).

Library of Congress Cataloging-in-Publication Data

Mosley, Steven R., 1952-
  Secrets of the mustard seed : ten life-changing promises from the New
Testament / Steven Mosley.
    p. cm.
  ISBN 1-57683-317-8
  1. Christian life. I. Title.
  BV4501.3 .M675 2002
  248.4--dc21

                              2002002124

Printed in the United States of America

2 3 4 5 6 7 8 9 10 / 06 05 04 03 02

FOR A FREE CATALOG OF
NAVPRESS BOOKS & BIBLE STUDIES,
CALL 1-800-366-7788 (USA)
OR 1-416-499-4615 (CANADA)

Contents

The WAY OF LOVE

WHILE THE Beatles were doing a little soul searching in India, John Lennon insisted on going up in a helicopter ride with the Maharishi, hoping that, somehow, while airborne, the guru would let him in on the secret: the meaning of life. But the Maharishi just commented on the scenery.

Cecil Adams, who made quite a name for himself as "the world's smartest human being," provided a service in his nationally syndicated column: "All major mysteries of the cosmos succinctly explained." But when people wrote in for "The Straight Dope" they could only get answers to questions like, "Do turkeys really drown when they look up during rainstorms?" And "Do you get better gas mileage with the air conditioner on or with the windows open?" When it came to "How can I be happy?" Cecil was a bit short on advice.

Pierre Gassendi had quite a lot to say during his life as a professional philosopher. So when loved ones huddled around his deathbed they were hoping for some final revelation. He mumbled, "I was born without knowing why; I am dying without knowing why."

Great words of advice don't fall on us easily. When we want

7

something beyond "Always eat your spinach" or "Do one thing at a time," things get pretty fuzzy. That's why people go to extraordinary lengths to find something they can hang on to.

Americans on a "spiritual adventure" tour are flown halfway around the world to Egypt so they can descend through narrow, torch-lit passageways under the 2.3 million granite blocks of the Great Pyramid of Khufu. Arriving at the King's Chamber, they lie one by one in the bare sarcophagus and listen intently in the heavy silence for some echo of ancient insight that might enlighten their souls. After such travels the typical sentiment is, "I came seeking wisdom and all I got was this T-shirt." The mystery remains.

Something quite different happens when you discover the New Testament. If you want to know what it's all about, this document tells you in plain language. It doesn't play coy. It doesn't wrap it in a riddle.

Jesus gives us life in a nutshell. His principle word of wisdom came in response to a question posed by his religious rivals, the Pharisees: What is the greatest commandment? These religious leaders had an extraordinary amount of advice to give people about how to live. Their tradition multiplied divine precepts into countless laws about the details. Jesus, however, condensed his advice into a single verb—love: "'Love the Lord your God with all your heart and with all your soul and with all your mind.' This is the first and greatest commandment. And the second is like it: 'Love your neighbor as yourself.' All the Law and the Prophets hang on these two commandments."

Developing a full life is about developing love. Jesus' great summary of the law expands on that verb. He was saying, in effect, when it comes to knowing God, we don't get it until we give it up. Casual gestures made toward his extravagant grace only immunize us to its potency. God asks us to respond in kind. Not halfheartedly. Not absentmindedly. But soul-ed out. So love on your tiptoes, taking in your breath, like you've seen the Grand Canyon for the first time and awe makes you tumble into something so much vaster than yourself.

Jesus was also saying, when it comes to relationships, we don't grow until we give it up. Extending token bits of charity to our neighbors only keeps them at a safe distance. God asks us to reach out to people as if we were trying to find ourselves in them, as if their well-being were our own.

Love is the queen of New Testament virtues. Jesus always spotlighted it: "This is my command: Love each other." John celebrated it: "Whoever loves his brother lives in the light." Paul crowned it again: "The entire law is summed up in a single command: 'Love your neighbor as yourself.'"

Love is what people need to find up in a helicopter with a guru or at the bottom of a pyramid. Love transforms everything. Without love nothing really changes; our best efforts are just clanging cymbals.

Without love we try to fill holes. With love we overflow.

Without love we put up a good front. With love we have faces.

Without love we hoard approval. With love we share delight.

Without love we manipulate. With love we ask.

Without love we claw to the top. With love we rule from the bottom.

Without love we manufacture more religion. With love we respond with more faith.

Without love we throw stones from a glass house. With love we build on a solid rock.

Love is the best advice you'll ever get. But love, of course, is only a word. Sometimes circumstances drain it of content. Sometimes betrayals reduce it to four letters.

That's why Jesus and his apostles have a lot to say about the Way of Love. Some of us may feel a bit out of the loop when it comes to loving in a healthy way. The New Testament shows us how to get in. It shows us how to cultivate this essential seed of life. It shows us how it can blossom into a tree bearing all kinds of fruit. It shows us how we can nourish ourselves and others with it. And it does this by turning simple, mustard-seed-size words of advice into life-changing promises.

If you look at the New Testament carefully, you'll discover ten things Jesus and the apostles urge us to do the most. These admonitions stand out when you simply zero in on the words they used most frequently. They stand out when you look for phrases that give special emphasis to a precept—do this more and more; do this as opposed to something else. They stand out when you look at the passages in which New Testament writers make their most passionate appeals.

By using these three criteria I've come up with the New Testament's top ten words of advice. They are essentially the New Testament's Ten Commandments. The Old Testament Ten Commandments are prohibitions. They serve as moral boundaries, showing us where we don't want to go. And that's important. But even more important are principles that show us where we *do* want to go. These new principles show us how rich life can be inside those boundaries.

These are simple, basic commands that show us how to fulfill the essential law of love. But so much life, so much wisdom, is packed into those phrases. Hidden away inside them we can find Mustard Seed Secrets, promises that can dramatically improve the quality of our lives. They are small steps we can take that yield the biggest results.

Jesus liked to describe his kingdom as a tiny mustard seed, which grows into a wide, shady tree. In that striking picture he spotlights the kingdom of heaven as a living thing that greatly expands our lives. It can turn something small and insignificant into something bountiful and glorious.

These Mustard Seed Secrets show us exactly how the kingdom works that way, how the Way of Love works that way. The power of the mustard seed lies in these New Testament words of wisdom. I invite you to follow them, step by step, into the abundant life that Jesus promised.

Cited:

Greatest commandment—Matthew 22:37-40
My command—John 15:17
Live in the light—1 John 2:10
The entire law—Galatians 5:14
Kingdom as a mustard seed—Matthew 13:31;
    Mark 4:31; Luke 13:19

CHAPTER ONE

BY FAITH

Make more of you by setting up a rendezvous

SOMEBODY cranked up the volume. Somebody pressed fast-forward. Have you noticed? The world is getting a lot more intense, more demanding. Companies rise and fall with the speed of Internet access. We're phoned and faxed and e-mailed and paged and overnight-delivered a flood of requests that find us wherever we are. And we have to respond in kind—or fall behind.

Even at home we often turn to multitasking just to keep up. What two or three things can you do at once? Take the girls to Little League and run to the grocery store during innings when they're not up to bat? Throw signs at your fifth-grader to keep off the Nintendo and concentrate on his homework while you're doing the dishes and phoning someone to baby-sit this weekend? Or maybe it's just coming home Friday after another long day at work, collapsing in a heap on the couch—and then remembering the fix-it and clean-up chores that have been piling up since Monday.

At some point most of us want to scream, "There's just not enough of me to go around!" If only we could reproduce ourselves. After all, clones are people two. Or maybe we could use three or four.

Well, the New Testament offers a remarkable solution to our problem, not through genetic engineering, but through a simple word to the wise that has enormous potential: live by faith. Christ's apostles actually claim that faith can make more of you. Faith stands out as the quality the New Testament mentions the most—483 references to faith, belief, believe. Jesus pointed the lame, the blind, the proud, and the broken to it as their only hope. The apostles centered their gospel around it.

Furthermore, they tell us that something extraordinary happens when we do live by faith. In Ephesians Paul promised that Christ can live in our hearts through faith. And because Christ is "the fullness of the Deity," we weak, mistake-prone human beings can be "filled to the measure of all the fullness of God."

The faith connection we make with God is far more potent than fiddling with DNA. It makes more of us in a most spectacular way—spreading us out into "the fullness of God."

It's not just, as Jesus said, that a mustard seed of faith can uproot trees or move mountains into the sea (as if that wasn't enough). Living by faith actually multiplies us; we get to tap into God's omnipotence and omnipresence. That's a life-changing promise. That's the great Mustard Seed Secret of faith.

Sounds fantastic. But how does this work in the real world? In the fast-tracked, high-tech present, people are much more likely to live by their wits. We live by the laws of science. We live defensively. We're not tending sheep by still waters and green pastures. How do we accomplish more if we're looking up? Options whiz by us every second and we can fall behind by just blinking.

Try an experiment: set up a rendezvous. First, spot a need. Maybe it's something on your long to-do list—your spouse is depressed, your child is having conflicts at school, you have to find

a new job. Then brainstorm a bit about how God might meet that need. What's a solution? What's the first step from here to there? Pray about how you can cooperate with God's efforts. Finally, set up that rendezvous. Ask to meet God and his resources at the point of that need. Prayerfully decide to become part of the solution.

It's really just a simple, small, mustard-seed step. But I've been amazed over and over by how providences multiply as soon as I go where I'm asking God to go. He somehow amplifies prayerful action and I find there's enough of me to go around.

Setting up a rendezvous means you don't go out there alone and try to play the part of rescuer. You don't assume you have to make everyone happy. Instead, you respond to what God is nudging you to do; you cooperate with what he's up to.

Setting up a rendezvous makes more of you without taking more out of you. You don't get drained trying to keep up with all those needs out there. You're plugged into inexhaustible resources.

I was teaching at a Christian language school in Japan when I first caught a sense of this kind of providential meeting. Early one morning, I felt moved to pray for something to happen — really happen. I'd just read a few pointed verses in one of Paul's epistles on loving and serving one another. Tired of generic resolves to be nice, of sliding through days without any ripple, I felt an urge to take God from my devotions out into the next sixteen waking hours. Surely somewhere in my day there must be a specific rendezvous with his will.

So I said, "Lord, lead me to someone I can really help today." It was not your everyday nod toward goodness. I wanted to be aimed at a target.

My morning classes passed uneventfully. But after staff meeting, a teacher named Peggy stopped me in the hallway. "I need to talk to you," she said with unsettling directness. "Can we go somewhere?"

We entered an unoccupied classroom and she spilled the beans: "I feel like a total fake. I don't even know why I'm here as a missionary." Peggy unleashed a flood of insecurity and inadequacy that was welling up from a chaotic childhood. This adult English teacher dissolved into a hurting, fearful little girl.

Some of us had written off Peggy as one of those loud, graceless types that you just have to tolerate. Not exactly the prom queen. But now I found myself looking past the packaging.

Nothing like this had ever happened to me before. I'd never been much of a shoulder to cry on, just the old male cliché: doing my own thing, live and let live, content with work and an occasional game of football.

But now I was so excited about having reached the rendezvous with the person whom God wanted me to contact that I did become all ears. I did try to understand Peggy's longings and frustrations. And I even managed to get her started in a devotional study of the Bible that made her life a little more stable.

To my great surprise, other earfuls followed from other teachers. I became someone much more than myself—a counselor they trusted. There was more of me to go around because it was God's eagerness to help and heal that had built momentum inside me. We were on a roll together only because his skill at touching people was nudging me into places I'd never been.

God made more of me to go around. Part of the dynamic of setting up a rendezvous is that it focuses us on what God can do, not on what we can or can't do. We accomplish more because we work better when we're working with a creative, dynamic, positive individual.

When two blind men by a Galilean road accosted Jesus, he got them to focus on his power: "Do you believe that I am able to do this?" They did . . . and he did.

On another occasion, when a leper approached Jesus and said, "If you are willing, you can make me clean," the Master rewarded his faith immediately, restoring him to health.

Jesus wanted these individuals to affirm the fact that he could meet their needs. He wanted them to think about his abilities, and not just their disabilities. He wanted people looking not at how big (or small) their faith was, but at how big God is.

Faith helps to calm us—so we don't waste energy banging against a brick wall. Faith helps to focus us—so we don't get paralyzed by the problems. Faith connects us to a God who's simply bigger than our biggest challenges. He has an infinite number of solutions.

One blustery, stormy day, a farm boy named Raymond huddled in the family cellar with his trembling sister among the carrots and potatoes, listening as a tornado rampaged through Texarkana, littering its wake with telephone poles, livestock, and post offices. Raymond's eyes were glued to the rattling cellar door. He thought that at any second the storm would plunge in and drag him away.

The tornado passed and the boy survived. The homestead was repaired, and life resumed its slow, rhythmic pace. But the terror remained for Raymond. After that day, the very earth—which had once been so solid—seemed to expose him to the weather's violent whims. Every darkening of the sky, every gust of wind through the treetops, froze the boy's pulse. He could hardly function, shrinking inside a fear he thought would never leave him.

One Sunday, a visiting minister came to the white frame church two miles down the road. He spoke about the power of faith and prayer. He insisted that God is big enough to meet our smallest and greatest needs.

Raymond decided to try it out. Slipping off into the scrub oak woods by himself, he looked into the sky that had gone berserk and told God he was awfully tired of this fear and would he, Sir, mind taking it away from him? Then he went back to plowing the cornfield.

A few days later, Raymond realized he hadn't felt afraid since making his petition in the woods. A few gray clouds had gone by, the wind had picked up a couple of times, but that acid fear in his stomach was gone. It seems that God had simply dissolved it, without benefit of progressive desensitization, positive thinking, or any other mental exercise.

Some years later, Raymond found himself on a Navy ship in the middle of the Pacific. A fierce storm came up and quickly lashed the sea into wild gyrations. Fifty-foot waves exploded against the taut steel of his troop carrier. As the fury of the squall mounted and the ship swayed and pitched, everyone fled below deck. Only a few officers remained on the bridge trying to hold the ship on course.

Everyone fled, that is, except Raymond. Soaked with spray that shot high in the air from the roller-coastering bow, this sailor hung tightly to the upper deck railing. He found himself enjoying the storm immensely. His own youthful energies, cramped for so long aboard ship, seemed to shout with the forces clashing from horizon to horizon. It was exhilarating. The untamed animation of sky, wind, and water left him breathless.

It seemed like a mid-ocean rendezvous with God's majesty and omnipotence. That's what he was celebrating. In contrast to the false bravado of men below deck psyching themselves up for battle, Chief Yeoman Raymond Mosley, my father, felt awed and humbled before the vast drama around him.

Faith expands us in all "the fullness of God." Faith makes more of us.

When storms threaten, faith lifts a sail.

When gloom descends, faith lights a candle.

When "can't do" rules, faith creates a "can do" coup.

When loneliness stretches to the horizon, faith taps into the height and breadth and depth of God's love.

The writer of Hebrews celebrates ordinary men and women who accomplished great things by faith, people "whose weakness was turned to strength," people who "quenched the fury of the flames," people of whom the world was not worthy, who were "longing for a better country—a heavenly one." They are a cloud of witnesses above us, cheering us on. They're telling us that we can be part of this glorious heritage; we too, by faith, can do great things for God.

I heard that calling one night in my living room. I heard it

through my father's voice as he read Scripture. There was something about that voice that got to me.

A few nights before, I had happened to catch my baby's voice in the still of the evening. I'd just put my daughter in her crib and was about to work on a script at my computer. But then I stopped. She was cooing. She was talking in that language before language, throwing out sounds just for the pleasure of it. And in this child's guileless voice I heard the goodness of God.

It was new, like something at creation, and so very contented. I imagined her to be instinctively living by faith. And I knew how precious this human being really was.

Then came another still evening. I picked up Dad's voice from the guest bedroom. Speaking with great difficulty, he was reading one of Paul's epistles to my stepmother. A year before, my father had suffered a massive stroke that left him partially paralyzed. It had taken months of therapy for him to be able to speak again, and even now the words didn't come easily; they were always taking detours in his brain; he had to track them down.

But Dad still wanted to taste the Word of God in his mouth; he wanted to form the words of faith out loud. So he struggled to get out each phrase, each one of Paul's descriptions of a glorious Savior. Sometimes he strained to grunt the syllables together. But there was also a gentleness in his voice.

I listened almost without breathing. This was my father's faith ringing out in the dark. It made him larger than life. This was the man who stood on the deck of the ship as it bucked in a mid-ocean storm. This was the man who had replaced fear with a trust in the unbounded Almighty.

For me, my daughter's cooing and my Dad's reading formed wonderful bookends that encompassed all there is to say about trusting God. I realized that I want faith to be there with me at the beginning and I want faith to be there at the end. That's the only way to live. It's the Way of Love.

My father died a year later, but I can still hear his voice. And I still want to join him in that great cloud of witnesses.

When I fail miserably, I want to turn my face in faith to God.

When it's dark, I want to speak about the light that illuminates every child born into this world.

When I'm hurting, I want to affirm my allegiance to the One who took on our afflictions.

When I'm confused, I want to praise the wisdom of the heavenly Father anyway.

When I'm angry, I want to acknowledge the love that won't let me go.

When I feel misunderstood or betrayed, I want to give thanks for the One who sees into my innermost being.

And I want to send all the joys of my life up to the One who is the source of every good and perfect gift.

Yes, I want to live by faith.

Cited:

Christ lives in hearts by faith — Ephesians 3:17
The measure of all the fullness — Ephesians 3:19
The fullness of God — Colossians 1:19; 2:9-10
Uproot trees — Luke 17:6
Move mountains — Mark 11:23
Believe I am able — Matthew 9:28
If you are willing — Mark 1:40
Heroes of faith — Hebrews 11:16,32-40

Overflow WITH THANKS

Lighten your world by opening the aperture of your heart

THE RAGGED European internees standing in rows in the center of Shantung Compound feared the worst as the Japanese chief of police prepared to read his verdict.* They'd heard rumors of atrocities in other prisoner-of-war camps in China, and this was the first opportunity for their captors to demonstrate real retribution.

The "criminal" standing beside the Japanese officer was a small, bespectacled Catholic named Father Darby. He'd been caught slipping eggs under his cassock as he prayed by the compound wall. Father Darby, it turned out, was a key link between sympathetic Chinese villagers outside and the starving inmates.

The chief began his speech in a loud voice, declaring that he was determined to stamp out the black market and would have to

---

* This story is a paraphrase of one recorded by Langdon Gilkey in *Shantung Compound* (New York: Harper & Row, 1966), pp. 37-38.

21

make an example of Father Darby, even though it pained him to punish "a man of the cloth." The weary listeners shuddered; would this gentle father be tortured or only shot? The chief announced, "I sentence you to one and a half months of solitary confinement!"

There was a moment's pause and then the internees erupted in a cheer that shocked the solemn Japanese official. Father Darby, they knew, had served as a Trappist monk, thriving in the silence and solitude of the same monastery for twenty-five years. And so, as Japanese soldiers shook their heads, the father marched off to his tiny dark cell . . . humming a hymn.

Solitary confinement would have been a terrible ordeal for most of the people languishing in Shantung Compound. But Father Darby took it as a spiritual opportunity. The only difference between hellish isolation and heavenly peace was his attitude, the way he'd come to regard such an experience.

Some time ago, William James wrote, "The greatest discovery of my generation is that a human being can alter his life by altering his attitude." Today mental-health professionals hammer away at the point: it's not what happens to us that determines the quality of our lives; it's how we interpret what happens to us that counts. Life doesn't come to us directly; it's mediated through our point of view, our mindset, our assumptions.

There's one attitude in particular that comes through strong and clear in the New Testament. It's emphasized sixty-two times: the attitude of thankfulness. Most people can be persuaded to say a few words of thanksgiving when the skies are blue and a new sedan is in the garage. But the apostles urge us to express thanks even when it's raining cats and dogs and the old clunker is at the shop. Paul advised the Thessalonians: "Give thanks in all circumstances, for this is God's will for you in Christ Jesus." He urged the Ephesians: "Sing and make music in your heart to the Lord, always giving thanks to God the Father for everything." He told the Colossians that life in Christ should overflow with thankfulness.

Give thanks always. Give thanks in all circumstances. This is a specifically Christian innovation. The fact is, nothing else we do can change our surroundings more dramatically or more quickly. Thanksgiving transforms our world. That's a life-changing promise. That's a Mustard Seed Secret. To radically change your environment, you don't have to wait for a government program. You don't have to move to another state or country. It can happen here and now.

One day I was directing some segments for *Still Standing True,* a television series about biblical heroes of faith. But I just couldn't get Moses to look heroic. We were shooting the actor from various angles—Moses on a rock, gesturing with his staff; Moses pleading and praying against a spotless blue sky. But everything seemed too literal, too plain as day.

Finally, I asked my director of photography to put the camera on the ground, shoot up toward Moses against the sun, and open up the f-stop—go ahead, blow it out. And suddenly there it was—a man grappling in the desert with El Shaddai himself! That's what I was trying to get across. Stretching out his limbs, this figure blurred into the light as if he were being propelled toward the glory of God.

All we needed was to open up the f-stop, to let more light in. That seemed to take us all the way to the Promised Land. The landscape hadn't changed at all. The sun was still shining down with exactly the same illumination. But a simple change of aperture in the camera lens transformed the scene. Sagebrush turned golden. Scrub oaks danced in refracted rays. Ordinary sunlight flared into a visionary haze.

Giving thanks is powerful simply because it lets more light in. It functions like an aperture—the aperture for our hearts. It may not seem like a very big thing. In fact it may seem as tiny as a mustard seed. But when it's opened up toward God, it can let in such a flood of light that our world is transformed.

An attitude of thanksgiving can dissipate the dark—both external and internal. That's why Jesus emphasized the importance of our outlook: "The eye is the lamp of the body. If your eyes are good, your whole body will be full of light. But if your eyes are bad, your whole body will be full of darkness. If then the light within you is darkness, how great is that darkness!"

When our eyes are good, when the apertures of our hearts are opened toward God, then our whole being can be flooded with light. God's light pouring in makes us stronger than all the darkness around us; it makes us more resilient than anything in the world that keeps blowing out candles.

Wonderful things happen when we let some of that light fall on our present circumstances. Thanksgiving counters the culture of complaint that greases so much interaction today. Sure, beefing about how bad things are is good for comic relief. But why make it a steady diet?

You either moan about slipping on the ice or give thanks it's holding you up.

You can gripe about the sunburn or give thanks for the skin cream.

You can whine about rain on your picnic or give thanks it's falling on your rosebuds.

You can complain you never have enough time or give thanks your life is so full.

It all comes down to what you choose to look at today. Why wail about all the terrible things happening in the world when you can give thanks for "the grace that is reaching more and more people" this very moment? Why major in "Satan's greatest deceptions" when you can appreciate God's clearest truths?

To give thanks in all circumstances we don't have to pretend that the world is safer than it is or that people are nicer than they are. We don't have to put blinders on to be thankful. We have to keep an eye out for blessings. God has sprinkled plenty of them around in the present. Paul said we can "live as children of light (for the fruit of the light consists in all goodness, righteousness and truth)." The sun's rays create an incredible variety of fruit. There are blueberries in the bushes; apples, nectarines, and mangoes in the trees. Opening ourselves to God's light can bear abundant fruit as well.

God creates with light. God uses the very act of thanksgiving to work good out of evil, redemption out of calamity. He's a Monet coloring the world. Flowers are poking up through the mud. Rainbows are flashing across gray skies.

When our days are measured by complaints, we end up trying to create with dark. We just move the smudges around. There's a reason scientists have been able to calculate the speed of light: It's extraordinarily useful. Lasers repair corneas, play music, and encode messages. But what's the speed of dark? Nobody knows because it's not going anywhere.

Giving thanks in all circumstances is a key part of walking "in the light, as he is in the light." God sees the good end from the sorry beginning. God sees his plans unfolding in the midst of the chaos of human history. Opening the aperture of our hearts gives him more room to work transformations.

Mike Riley dearly loved his new silver turbo-charged Porsche. When someone stole the sports car, he was dismayed. By the time police tracked it down, the vehicle had been stripped and gutted.

Mike felt terrible, but on the way to the junkyard he got an idea. Instead of just dumping his beloved wreck there, he had them crush the vehicle into a two-by-three-foot cube. It now serves as a coffee table in his living room, and he serves drinks from custom hubcaps.

Mike's root beer may taste a bit greasy, but he teaches us something important about troubles: Turn them into something else! Turn the car wreck into a coffee table.

Yes, sometimes bad things do happen to us. Sometimes we do have reasons to complain. But that's when we need to let in more light. Why? Because thanksgiving permits God to compress the problem into some useful shape. Our human instinct is to expand on misfortune. We tend to get stuck in the junkyard moaning about how beautiful our Porsche used to be. God wants to give us a ride home. He has something to teach us. He wants to help us find a way out of our disappointment.

One of the ways thankfulness overflows beautifully in the New Testament is in the way its writers thanked God for other people. You see this in the first part of almost every epistle. Paul's greeting to the Philippians, for example—how would you like to receive this note: To think of you is to thank God for you. To pray for you is to pray with joy.

The apostles always made it a point to focus on the good qualities they saw in believers. That's another way God creates with light. The congregations they shepherded had plenty of difficulties and conflicts. But that's overshadowed by this wonderful spirit of thankfulness. It's one of the things that bound these early believers so tightly together.

How we view other people's differences makes a big difference. This is important because the people who irritate us the most often have the most to teach us. What they have too much of, we usually need more of.

We can complain about the blabbermouth next door or give thanks that he can show us how to loosen up a bit.

We can talk trash about our lazy coworker or give thanks that she can help us be less driven and compulsive.

We can roll our eyes because of those irresponsible, unruly teenagers or thank God for their energy and spontaneity.

Giving thanks for other people can also shed light in another direction: backward. It can illuminate the past. Most of us have had an imperfect upbringing; we've been hurt or disappointed by our caregivers. And some of us spend much of our lives trying to fix the past in various ways.

Eventually, we have to learn that the past is one thing that can't be rewritten. At least we can't manipulate other people into making up for it. But what we can do is uncover a few blessings back there. It may take a little detective work, but finding things to be thankful for is worth the effort. Overall, the biblical history of Israel was a pretty sad affair. But God asked his people to memorialize the moments of great blessing.

All of us carry around the past as a very mixed bag. We know losses and we discover things we can learn. We experience injuries and we enjoy acts of kindness. What we choose to focus on can make an enormous difference. God does something great when we open the aperture of our hearts as we look back. Thanksgiving puts a laser beam in his hands and he's able to heal us in unique ways.

At the Osaka language school where I taught, a young woman named Yasuko was carrying around emotional baggage that went back three generations. Her wealthy great-grandmother had delegated the children to servants. Her grandmother had given her seven-year-old daughter away to a sister. In turn, Yasuko's mother simply didn't have the resources to nurture her.

This was a family that passed down bitter memories of abandonment. Yasuko's mother often recalled what it was like to go to the train station every day after school, peering in windows as passenger cars rolled in, hoping against hope that the woman who'd given her away would suddenly appear with repentant tears and sweep her up in a warm embrace.

The hug that never came was Yasuko's heritage. Her mother remained absent, emotionally and physically, for most of Yasuko's childhood. And her father had died shortly after World War II when Yasuko was only two. His main legacy seemed to be the drink fests he'd thrown at home for his comrades from the Manchurian front.

There didn't seem to be anything remotely admirable in Yasuko's roots that she could grab hold of. But after this young woman became a Christian, she decided to look more carefully. Starting a relationship with a heavenly Father who loved her unconditionally had opened her heart a bit; she felt ready to throw some of his light backward.

One evening, one of her dad's war buddies came by to pay his respects. And Yasuko started asking him questions. What did he like the most about her dad? The man chuckled, recalling the wild parties. And then he said, "You know, it was the funniest thing, by the end of the night he was so drunk he started shoving bags of rice and vegetables into our hands as we left. All kinds of things. He just about emptied the kitchen—didn't know what he was doing. But that fool saved our lives. The country was just devastated after the war. There were no jobs, almost no food. Some of us were starving."

After the man left, it was Yasuko's mother who was laughing. She said, "Actually, your father never drank a drop. He had a bad stomach. But he always had a glass in his hand and pretended to gulp down the *sake* just to be polite."

Yasuko thought about this for several days and then woke up in the middle of the night, startled by what her dad had actually done. Those men of her father's generation would have been humiliated by handouts. Even in desperate straits, becoming dependent on the pity of others was terribly dishonorable. But if some drunken fool started throwing gifts at you—that was another matter.

This revelation struck at something deep in Yasuko's heart. Her family had always been terribly concerned about what other people thought. They constantly struggled to cover insecurity with the right appearances. But this man, her father, had shown real courage—throwing away his reputation for the sake of his comrades.

Seeing this also gave her a whole new appreciation for the Christ who had gone to the cross, freely discarding his spotless reputation as the Son of God and taking on the appearance of a criminal.

Yasuko had found a reason to give thanks from the heart. And that shed a warmer light on the past that had always haunted her. The car wreck was turning into a coffee table. She started to believe she could pass on a very different legacy.

Wonderful things really do happen when we let God create with light.

Cited:

In all circumstances—1 Thessalonians 5:18
For everything—Ephesians 5:19-20
Overflowing—Colossians 2:7
Lamp of the body—Matthew 6:22-23
Grace reaching more and more—2 Corinthians 4:15
Fruit of light—Ephesians 5:8-9
Walking in the light—1 John 1:7
Thank God for you—Philippians 1:3-4

CHAPTER THREE

THE TRUTH

Hang on to what you have by reaching out for more

AT THE age of nineteen, I found myself one of fourteen thousand students attending Western Illinois University, walking to classes between twenty-story dormitories, an anonymous sophomore on a huge campus. I sat in lecture halls where agnostic science teachers talked about the origin of life and atheist literature professors talked about the meaning of life, or lack thereof.

I'd grown up learning memory verses in church school, tucked safely away from "the enticements of the world." And so the question was, would I be able to hold on to "biblical truth" in this new environment? Would my faith be swept away in this vast secular tide?

There was a part of me that hoped to get swept away. I didn't want to be stuck in a little religious corner of the world all my life. Church was feeling pretty cramped at the time.

The challenge I faced is the challenge all of us face on occasion—in school, at work, sometimes even at home. How do you retain your faith in a faithless environment? All of us who are parents think and pray about that a lot. Will our kids keep their faith?

Back home, people at the local church tried to help me hold on to my heritage. And they did it by reminding me, regularly, how much more truth our church had than anybody else. Of course, we had more truth than the people smoking pot and fornicating. But we also had more truth than any other Christian group that might try to seduce me away from our denomination.

The pastor, a kindly older gentleman, emphasized that point. "We've been given so much light. Other people have so little. So, hang on to what you've got."

As it turned out, I did manage to hang on to my faith during my years at Western Illinois. But it wasn't because I was reassured by those dear people at my local church. It was because my faith was stretched in ways I could not have imagined when I walked onto that campus.

Some kids in Campus Crusade for Christ befriended me, invited me to a retreat, and involved me in their action groups. I stumbled into something called discipleship. I began learning things about witnessing and a devotional life and the Holy Spirit that I had never picked up in my home church setting. And more importantly, I began practicing the Christian life in ways I hadn't before. Sharing my faith in those drug-infested high-rise dorms throbbing with the sounds of Woodstock, I discovered God really did have answers for the longings of a nineteen-year-old kid.

What I realize, looking back, is that I did hang on to my old faith, the faith of my childhood, because I was learning so many new things. I was pushed in all kinds of new directions spiritually, and that helped me get in touch with the basics of why I believed in God, in Scripture, in Jesus Christ as Lord.

The closest I ever came to giving up on church completely was when I sat in my home church sanctuary, listening to the whiny little organ accompanying voices that kept saying how much more we had than everybody else.

The problem is, you get tired *just trying* to hold on tight to the faith. Making a fist all the time wears you out! In fact, sometimes memorizing the truth can numb you to the truth. Just going over the same ground can sink you into a rut.

Truth is a big theme in the New Testament. Jesus and the apostles celebrate God's truth 109 times. And what's striking is that they always picture a truth greater than we are, a truth larger than life.

Paul happily affirmed that we can be chained up, but the Word can't. Peter wrote that we may be transient as grass, but God's truth stands forever. James claimed that we are born again through the word of truth. Jesus promised that the truth can set us free.

The New Testament, in other words, turns truth itself into a life-changing promise. Throughout Scripture we hear that God's thoughts are high above the earth, his word stands eternal in the heavens, his righteousness is like mighty mountains, and his judgments are like the great deep.

God's truth is bigger than we are. It's out there filling up the universe. We can't reduce it to anything inside us.

At the same time, the New Testament emphasizes another great principle. It may appear quite opposite: God's truth has to get inside us. If it doesn't get inside, it's not truth.

Jesus said that it was the Spirit who would lead us into all truth. John went so far as to say, "The Spirit is the truth." And the Spirit, of course, is God working inside us.

When Paul urged us to grow in truth, he talked about grasping the height and depth and breadth of Christ's love; he prayed that the eyes of our hearts may be enlightened. Truth must be written on our hearts and minds, something we feel and experience.

So there we have it. Two principles. The truth that sets me free has got to be bigger than me. It can't just be what feels right — me making up the rules as I go along. At the same time it has to be something I feel, something that lives in my heart.

How do we put these two things together? Think of oxygen.

God's truth functions like oxygen for the soul. To nourish us it has to come from the outside. We can't keep breathing in what we exhale for long. The air we need is created by the vast atmosphere circling this earth. But that air has to get into our lungs. Its molecules have to mix with our blood molecules. If it remains only external, something I nod at regularly but don't absorb, then I suffocate.

That's why the New Testament gives us a great Mustard Seed Secret: we hang on to what we have by reaching out for more. Bible writers don't tell us to *possess* the truth; they urge us to *love* the truth. Paul pointed out that many people had lost their way in life because they "refused to love the truth and so be saved." Jesus often advertised teachable children as model citizens of the kingdom to those who tried to capture and quantify "the truth." Peter urged believers to "crave pure spiritual milk" like newborn babies.

To love the truth is to keep learning. Truth isn't something you acquire, like jewelry. You don't show it off and then lock it away in a safe place. Truth is something that has to keep flowing in to keep you alive. You have to keep breathing.

We don't hang on to what we have by making a fist. We hang on by reaching out for more.

How do you know if you love the truth? Check out what happens when you disagree with it. What if the truth isn't on your side? What if the facts contradict your opinions? What if you find certain texts in the Bible that don't quite fall your way?

A drunk stumbling along a bar stopped before an enormous stuffed tarpon hanging on the wall. Squinting his eyes in amazement, he announced, "The fella who caught that fish is a liar!" When a truth doesn't fit into your frame of reference, something has to give.

The disciples hauled in an enormous catch of Galilee fish one afternoon after obeying Christ's instructions to cast their nets on the other side of the boat. They had to accept the fact that this wandering rabbi knew more about their profession than they did.

Make sure it doesn't require major surgery to get a new idea into your head. The greatest obstacle to the truth is not ignorance; it's human pride. What we need most is to remain teachable.

Pride filters out. The teachable listen in.

Pride narrows its gaze. The teachable welcome surprise.

Pride knows all the answers. The teachable ask questions.

Pride nurtures blind spots. The teachable go to where the light is.

Pride memorizes the letter of the law. The teachable get the Spirit.

Pride accumulates truth as ammunition for argument—and shoots itself in the foot. The teachable absorb truths that pierce the heart—and heal old wounds.

Loving the truth means we follow something bigger than us—wherever it leads. We have to keep breathing in this ocean of fresh air, this uncontainable Word of God.

Try this. When you get up in the morning, ask God to teach you something you don't know. Ask God to awaken you with the listening ear of a disciple. Move beyond nodding to the familiar, beyond checking off the right facts. What can you see today that you've been overlooking? Who could you listen to today whom you haven't heard?

That simple act of opening yourself up to learn is a mustard seed that will expand into a great, shady tree. You can lose so many impediments, so much baggage, when you listen to the God who searches our innermost hearts.

That helps you do something else that's equally therapeutic: speak the truth. The New Testament emphasizes the fact that honesty sets us free. Paul encouraged us to "put off falsehood and speak truthfully to [our] neighbor, for we are all members of one body." He maintained that we grow up into Christ by "speaking the truth in love." Writing to a group plagued by acrimonious lawsuits and incest, he called out, "We have spoken freely to you, Corinthians, and opened wide our hearts to you . . . As a fair exchange—I speak as to my children—open wide your hearts also."

We can unleash enormous energy in our lives just by being transparent with God and with people we can trust. Wonderful things happen when we trust the truth, when we stop being afraid of it. We could so much better invest the energy we expend trying to keep things hidden. One big reason we can't inhale fresh air—that oxygen for the soul—is that we haven't truly exhaled. We haven't removed the tired stuff.

Recently, I decided to interview both counselors and their counselees for a TV series called *Truths That Change Us Inside.* And what these people said over and over was that opening up proved liberating. Only open hearts heal. There's always pressure in any group to put on a good front. Those pressures only seem to intensify in the church. But risking honesty is one of the most powerful investments we can make. It's such a relief to finally exhale.

The closed memorize their smiles. The honest look you in the eye.

The closed pretend everything's okay. The honest know it's okay to be imperfect.

The closed try to be someone else. The honest are known for who they are.

The closed sit on the truth. The honest feel the weight of conviction.

The closed stifle the noise inside. The honest can relax in silence.

The closed conceal their mistakes and multiply them. The honest admit their faults and divide them.

The closed are always running from an interrogation. The honest want to hear even what is tough to hear.

One day a fellow English teacher in Japan named Rita slumped into my apartment and stared at the soggy, gray lumps of granola spread on the kitchen table. I was concocting a way to never grow hungry in a neighborhood stocked only with octopus, squid, and seaweed. She was dangling on the end of her rope.

The story came out in little bursts. She felt like a failure as a teacher. And in the Bible classes we taught, she just wasn't getting

anything across. Rita had begun to wonder if she even knew who this Christ was that she was always blabbing about.

I remembered Rita from the first day of classes at the school—trembling in the hallway, taking a deep breath before entering the classroom. I didn't think they made people this wide-eyed and innocent anymore. She'd put up a good front for a few months, but now she just had to be honest. Her darkest doubts about herself and God came tumbling out.

Anyone else sitting there, staring down at Little Orphan Annie hands, would have to be faking it. But I knew Rita's frailty went to the bone. She came from a very dysfunctional family plagued by incest.

We talked for a long time. Rita ended up agreeing to try a method of listening to God through the Word that had helped me a lot: Observation, Interpretation, Application. I assured her that God wanted very much to teach her individually and to do great things through her. She promised to start writing down what she learned each day.

All that week I prayed God would make Scripture come alive in her hands, sparking new insights, creating new abilities. And Rita began to absorb stimulating truths. One morning she shared something exciting she'd seen in Jesus' forgiveness of the woman caught in adultery, something to admire. I thought Rita's cheeks looked rosier than usual. Her eyes flickered a bit. She was definitely getting some fresh air.

Rita kept learning—and sharing. And slowly she developed the sense that she'd acquired a private tutor—yes, God was speaking to her.

At the time, all of us teachers were laboring with one student, Junko, who wanted to become a Christian but kept getting hung up on hypocrites in the church. We had all encouraged her to stop looking at people and to focus on Christ, but we weren't getting through. Then Rita had a talk. She told Junko . . . to stop looking at people and focus on Christ. Bam! Junko saw the light: "Yes, that's exactly what I need to do!" Little helpless Rita carried the day.

Nothing is more exciting than to watch God empower the weak. Rita was taking off. Her devotional life blossomed. She began wielding the Word in Bible classes to great effect. She was speaking confidently to businessmen and college students. Many of the disinterested began to take a second look.

Then Rita's emotionally disturbed sister came over to Japan for a visit. Their relationship had always been difficult because of abuse in the home. But now Rita became the healer. Sharing with her sister what she'd been learning, Rita helped this embittered young woman believe in something better. One day Rita's sister whispered, "I want what you guys have." Little Orphan Annie had struck it rich.

Cited:

The Word unchained—2 Timothy 2:9
Stands forever—1 Peter 1:24-25
Born again—James 1:18
Set us free—John 8:32
God's thoughts are high above the earth—Isaiah 55:9
Word eternal in the heavens—Psalm 119:89
Righteousness like mighty mountains—Psalm 36:6
Judgments like the great deep—Psalm 36:6
Lead us to truth—John 16:13
God's Spirit is truth—1 John 5:6
Height and depth of love—Ephesians 3:18
Eyes of heart enlightened—Ephesians 1:18
Crave spiritual milk—1 Peter 2:2
Put off falsehood—Ephesians 4:25
Speaking truth in love—Ephesians 4:15
Opened wide our hearts—2 Corinthians 6:11,13

CHAPTER FOUR

Forgive
FOR GOOD

Move past hurts from a position of strength

SHE WAS staring at the bits of scrambled egg he'd left on the table. He was staring at the lipstick on her coffee cup. It was supposed to have been a leisurely Saturday breakfast on the patio. But the summer sun barely broke through the tense gloom around the couple.

It started with Jackie's little complaint about Shawn almost forgetting their anniversary.

He insisted he'd planned ahead for their dinner date. "I'm very, very sorry Le Rendezvous Restaurant turned out to be a dumpy café," he said, "but it wasn't spur of the moment."

"Well," Jackie acknowledged wryly, "at least you looked in the phone book for something special."

The tension remained. Old arguments about her never being satisfied and him never really trying lingered about the table like a grumpy waiter right before closing.

After a long silence she burst out, "Ya know, Shawn, I've *forgiven* you for flirting with that hotel clerk last spring. I've *forgiven* you for ignoring my friends at the barbecue in August. I've *forgiven* you for losing my favorite necklace and for shooting an entire vacation with no film in the camera. But . . . but . . . you're just not coming through!"

It took a while for Shawn to gather up his reply: "Jackie, I'm far from perfect, but is forgiveness something you put in the bank—hoping to cash in on it later?"

Forgive and forget. It's not that easy, is it? Not when you've really been disappointed. The wrongs others do to us are great at hide-and-seek. We let go with one hand while the other clutches something tightly behind our backs. And yes, sometimes we even put forgiveness in the bank. We're storing up credit, and there'd better be a payback—with interest.

Wouldn't it be nice to be able to forgive cleanly—wipe out those ugly feelings along with the formal debt? Wouldn't it be great if past hurts didn't come back to haunt us? Recent medical research has directly linked an inability to forgive with increased heart disease. I helped produce a TV series at Florida Hospital in Orlando where Christian physicians are actually reversing the symptoms of heart disease—like high blood pressure—by teaching patients how to forgive more effectively.

The New Testament has a lot to say about forgiveness. It touches on the subject eighty-four times. And it typically urges us to forgive as we've been forgiven. We are to forgive as Christ forgave us.

That is actually a great promise. In that command we're going to find one of the New Testament's more spectacular Mustard Seed Secrets. We're going to find how to forgive cleanly, how to forgive so you have peace instead of resentment down the road.

First, let's think about the kind of forgiveness Jesus offered. If we're supposed to forgive like him, what exactly did he extend to humanity from the cross?

More than anything else, it was a permanent pardon. Christ forgave with eternity in mind. He wiped out the debt of our sin.

He cancelled our transgressions. He covered us with his garment of righteousness. Jesus is the kind of God who throws our worst mistakes into the deepest part of the sea. Gone. Disappeared. Deep-sixed.

Of course that's what we all need to do. It would be absolutely wonderful if we could forgive for good. It would be great for our relationships; it would be great for the state of our hearts.

So what enabled Jesus to do that? How did he forgive, in order to forgive for good?

Jesus did something very important before he went to the cross. It's something we often overlook. He expressed anger. You find it laid out very vividly in Matthew 23, where he protests against whitewashed sepulchers full of greed and self-indulgence, blind guides leading the blind, and a brood of vipers shedding the blood of prophets. He expressed how outraged he was by the hypocrisy of those so desperately trying to kill him. He wanted to free people from their oppressive religiosity.

Jesus didn't forgive because he discounted sin. He talked fervently about how hurtful it is. The Godhead couldn't just wipe out transgressions by decree. Divine wrath had to be expressed in order for the atonement to work.

Expressing anger is one of the prerequisites of forgiving permanently. So we need to express our feelings instead of discounting them: *That was wrong. That really hurt me.* We don't have to whine endlessly or get abusive, but we do need to let the pain speak: *I didn't deserve that. That was really inappropriate.*

If we just ignore the hurt and try to smile our way through forgiveness, the pain will just come out in other ways. What we stuff in the bottom drawer will pop out of the top drawer when we least expect it.

To forgive without expressing anger or disappointment is to forgive from a position of weakness. You don't want to offend the person who wronged you, so you wave off an apology with, "That's okay."

You resent the way people are treating you but you've got to keep throwing out forgiveness—hoping for some kind of acceptance.

Forgiving from weakness only invites more hurt. It never quite catches up with the pain. Forgiving to make friends is like knocking out the outer walls of your house to create room for guests. Eventually, the roof collapses.

What we often miss when we think of Jesus hanging bloody on a cross is this: He forgave from a position of strength. He was really standing upright, making a spectacle of the human cruelty that made his sacrifice necessary. He wasn't shrugging off the hurt or excusing injustice. He'd exposed the ugly face of sin. He'd stood unmoved before his accusers and those who mocked him. It was his passionate protest that enabled him to forgive for good.

Forgiving from weakness submerges the hurt. Forgiving from strength dislodges the hurt.

Forgiving from weakness creates an unspoken debt. Forgiving from strength squares things eye to eye.

Forgiving from weakness is a way to get something. Forgiving from strength is a way to give something.

Forgiving from weakness waves a white flag. Forgiving from strength covers with a white garment.

There's something else that stands out about the way Jesus forgave from the cross. He forgave for good because he understood exactly who he was; he understood his role as the Messiah. Despite appearances, no one manipulated him into going to Golgotha. He wasn't trapped there by his enemies.

If you look carefully in the Gospels, you will find a suffering Servant who was very much in charge. He did a lot of talking back.

He told the mob that came to arrest him: "This has all taken place that the writings of the prophets might be fulfilled."

He let the high priest know who he was: "You will see the Son of Man sitting at the right hand of the Mighty One."

He let Pilate know who had fallen into his hands: "I am a king.

In fact, for this reason I was born, and for this I came into the world, to testify to the truth."

He let the thief crucified beside him in on the secret: "You will be with me in paradise."

The apostle John in particular presents Jesus as chief protagonist in the drama at Calvary. The Messiah makes every detail of the story echo his redemptive theme. The cross is a weapon he wields to pierce human hearts.

Yes, Christ was led as a lamb to the slaughter, but he didn't absorb the blows and lashes and nails because he thought he deserved it. He wasn't silent before his adversaries because he was intimidated, but because he was confident of his mission.

Jesus forgave so well because he knew who he was. He forgave from a position of strength. He forgave because he freely chose to do that.

That's how you can forgive for good: Know who you are. You are a child of God, cherished by a resourceful Savior. You deserve to be respected. You deserve to be loved.

You don't say, "Oh, it was nothing," when you're hurting. You don't forgive in order to score points or make people like you. Forgiving to find yourself is like trying to cover ugly graffiti with a thin coat of watercolor. You brush and brush; you slop on the weak mixture, but the obscenities still show through. It's hard work. You keep counting the number of times you've done it.

Forgiving because we know who we are is to paint with thick, red brush strokes. We don't have to keep trying. It's the potent mixture of Christ's kind of forgiving that enables us to wipe out those hurts, those wrongs. *It wasn't right. It wasn't fair. I didn't deserve it. But I choose to forgive—just as Jesus did.* When we forgive with this confidence, we can forgive and move on.

A good friend of mine told me how he finally took that step. Roland had been struggling through the aftermath of a divorce for several years, living in what he called "an upside-down world where true love gets its teeth knocked out and manipulation lives happily ever after." In other words, he resented all the ways he'd been an enabler in the relationship.

But one spring morning as the sun streamed through his bedroom window, Roland decided to have a no-holds-barred talk with God about his life (or lack thereof). In the middle of that conversation he suddenly realized he didn't want to be angry anymore.

Yes, working through the wreckage had been useful after the breakup. Yes, some venting had been therapeutic. But he didn't want to settle down in that neighborhood. He didn't want to become a hostile person who was always reacting to dysfunctionals, determined that "no one will ever do that to me again."

What mattered most was as clear at that moment as the light throwing patterns across his bedroom wall: "I wanted my life to center around love. I wanted to be moved by love. I wanted to get up in the morning because of love—not just as something I dream of having someday, but as something I show other human beings today."

"That's who I am!" he almost yelled at me when breaking the news. "At least that's who I want to be more than anything else."

A few days later Roland woke up with another bit of news in his head: it was time to forgive Katie, his ex-wife. Up until that moment, forgiveness just didn't register when it came to her. He understood the concept; he could talk with other people about its value. But for years he'd just felt a complete blank when it came to reaching out in any way to this person. All the ugly interaction with her was ancient history—like the family albums he'd stuffed into a paper sack in the back of his closet. He and Katie hadn't been able to agree on how to split up the pictures, so the albums just sat there in the dark, hostage to the couple's ill will.

But now Roland just had to say certain words. He picked up the phone to make the tough call, telling Katie he needed to forgive her and that he hoped she would be able to forgive him.

Some time after that brief conversation Roland retrieved those albums, made color copies of a stack of pictures at Kinko's, and drove to Katie's house to give her the originals. Back home, he began looking through his copies—the record of his children growing up—and the wonderful memories reduced him to tears.

My friend had come close to sinking into a bitter, middle-aged limbo. But rediscovering who he was moved him to forgive. He wasn't flailing about, trying to get his bearings anymore. He was forgiving from a position of strength.

There's one more thing that will help us forgive for good. It's something the New Testament emphasizes the most about our identity. Jesus pictures us as debtors who come before a king and fall on our faces, penniless. We plead our case, which is really no case at all. And the king graciously decides to wipe out the entire debt.

That's who we are: the forgiven, people who get off free. It's not just some lucky accident that bounces our way. It's not just a part of our story. It's our identity.

Every selfish and thoughtless act, every mistake, every mean gesture, every unkind word, every manipulative plan, every resentful day we've spent in our entire lives has been wiped off the record. That's Christ's gift from the cross. The whole weight of sin we've accumulated—and still accumulate—is met with a firm *Never happened. Don't know anything about it.*

So, having such divine pardon lavished on us, *of course* we don't demand reparation for every little wrong done to us, *of course* we don't go over and over that list of slights, *of course* we don't hold back forgiveness until we've extracted a pound of flesh.

Realizing that we've been forgiven much goes a long way toward enabling us to forgive others freely and cleanly. As Jesus said, he who has been forgiven much, loves much. Everybody has been forgiven much. It's just that some are more conscious of it than others. And that makes all the difference between stewing in the past and loving in the present.

Through his heroic sacrifice on the cross, Jesus did place forgiveness in the bank. But it's not something he plans on cashing in. It's something *we* cash in. It's ours to claim every day. It's ours to claim in the Judgment: complete pardon and acceptance.

Forgiveness is a self-reinforcing experience. The more we realize we are forgiven, the more we're able to forgive. And the more we forgive, the more we appreciate divine forgiveness. "Forgive, and you will be forgiven." Be forgiven and you'll forgive.

All her life, Marsha had heard about Christ's pardon and never knew quite what to do with it. Sure, it was a wonderful gesture, and she could say the right words about sin and grace and redemption. But someone shedding his blood for her small-town, nice-girl, home-by-ten mistakes? It seemed like overkill.

Then Marsha stumbled into a disastrous marriage and barely escaped with her life. Afterward, feeling frisky and rebellious, she determined to find out what it was like to make big-town, bad-girl, never-home mistakes. Marsha couldn't bring herself to actually frequent bars for one-night stands. But she did play the field at clubs, draw a following, and sample relationships.

Having exhausted the singles scene, she started going back to church. And there Marsha heard a very ordinary sermon on God's forgiveness that struck her to the marrow. She remembered a couple of faces—men she'd hurt very badly. She also remembered how she'd been spared from serious harm while in a Margarita daze with a limousine full of groping band members in the back streets of Los Angeles. God did seem like a gracious rescuer of the undeserving. The weight of his grace broke her heart. With tears streaming down her cheeks, Marsha understood for the first time in her life what it means to be forgiven.

Some weeks later, she found herself standing beside her ex-husband's pickup. She'd ushered her little boys inside the house while arguing with him, as usual, about his late child support. They quarreled a lot and there was a lot behind their quarrels. Marsha fiercely resented the way he'd been sexually insensitive in their marriage. She'd never been able to let it go. And now it all came up in one long blast.

To her surprise, John hung his head and said, "Yeah, I know. I'm sorry for that."

Marsha was surprised again when she replied, "I forgive you." These were words that had never been exchanged between them. But she recognized sincere regret in his face, and now she knew what that felt like.

Marsha began to sense her rock-hard anger dissolving, and one day she decided to ask her kids what they liked to do at Dad's house. They happily chattered about all kinds of things. Dad helped them build birdhouses and a hutch for their pet rabbits. Dad had decorated their bedroom like a pirate cove. Dad took them fishing and went on all the rides at Disneyland. Dad even made homework fun.

Why hadn't she seen this before? The mistreatment in the past was always making Marsha believe John was a total loser in the present. But now those dark deeds would not return to haunt her. She could thank God her boys enjoyed a good relationship with their father.

We are the forgiven. Those thick, red brush strokes cover the worst of our own mistakes. And that, more than anything else, is why we can forgive for good.

Cited:

Forgive as forgiven—Ephesians 4:32; Colossians 3:13
Into the depths of the sea—Micah 7:19
Prophets fulfilled—Matthew 26:56
At the right hand—Matthew 26:64
I am a king—John 18:37

In paradise—Luke 23:43
Seventy times seven—Matthew 18:22
A servant whose debt was cancelled—Matthew 18:21-35
Forgiven much—Luke 7:47
Forgive, be forgiven—Luke 6:37; Matthew 6:14

Encourage DAILY

Build healthier relationships with a musical language

WHEN I was five I developed the idea that there were man-eating chickens in the world. I suppose it started when a large white hen with an anger-management problem chased me around our Ford station wagon while the family was vacationing in Veracruz. I had unknowingly provoked the egg-layer, and she tore after me with wings waving. Screaming in terror, I ran around and around the car until someone shooed the fierce beast off.

This experience scarred me for life, of course. Chickens terrified me. Snakes were no problem. They were all there, muscular and firm. But who knew what mushy intestines might be concealed just underneath a fowl's feathers? I was deathly afraid of touching them.

I remember overhearing adults joke about a common irrational fear that some slimy reptile will creep up through the toilet and attack you when you least suspect. I knew I was alone among humanity—no one shared my burden of having to continually check for the aquatic rooster I was sure would someday shoot up through the plumbing as I sat down.

One day I tagged along with Dad to a farm just outside of town. I got caught up in him bargaining with the owner over the price of a horse and didn't notice that a flock of chickens was pecking its way toward us. Suddenly I looked down and saw to my horror that we'd become a tiny island surrounded by a vast sea of clucking hens.

How would I ever step through those hideous, jerking heads, those pointy beaks that could nail me to the ground forever? I was never going to get out alive.

Dad finally shook the farmer's hand and turned to go. My first test of manhood had come. And I was going to fail. But Dad looked down for the briefest moment, caught something in my eye, and took my hand. "Let's go home, Stevy," he said with a smile and then took a big step into the chickens. Those simple words fell on me like a magic wand. I could do this. I took a little step and the Red Sea parted. We walked right through the writhing horde on dry land.

Various things I learned about life in the fourth and fifth grades gave me the distinct impression that man-eating chickens are exceedingly rare on the earth. But I have never forgotten what Dad's words did for me.

It's remarkable the impact simple words of encouragement can have — especially when they touch the secret fears and insecurities no one else can see. All of us have moments when a good word can make a big difference. That's why the New Testament takes the words we utter very seriously. Jesus talked about casually cruel words following us into judgment. His apostles give us this exhortation over and over: Build up one another. Encourage one another. That's one piece of New Testament advice that stands out. We're to speak edifying words to each other daily, regularly, whenever we meet together.

Today we've become very sophisticated about dissecting words and relationships. We can analyze the dynamics behind codependence, dysfunction, and game playing. We can twist our psyches in all kinds of ways, trying to untie the knots made in childhood. And through all that we sometimes forget one basic fact: every day we create with our mouths the kinds of relationships we have.

Words are the raw material. Words can either tear down or build up. We can build healthy relationships just as surely as we can speak encouraging words. They are single notes we lay down here and there that may not seem like much, but taken together they create quite a melody.

So what's the secret to becoming a great encourager? How can our words have great influence for good? Some of us think we can't carry a tune when it comes to graciousness. Let me tell you about a friend of mine who should have been tone deaf.

Darryl's bedtime stories as he was growing up consisted of curses from the book of Deuteronomy. Those are the words he remembers. His father was so tyrannical and abusive that Darryl's younger brother fell apart emotionally at the age of eleven and had to be institutionalized.

Darryl grew up despising his father for what he'd done—and serving his father's God, an endlessly demanding deity. Throughout his teen years he felt isolated from his peers. Dating terrified him. Relationships of any kind were a strain. Darryl had very little chance of experiencing a normal life.

And yet, a couple of decades later when I got to know Darryl, he'd become a wonderfully nurturing father. We were both raising young children. Like most parents, I yelled too much, and I always noticed how calmly Darryl could defuse quarrels between his son and daughter. He had a wonderful way of dropping little words of encouragement on his kids, telling Krista why she would always be beautiful in his eyes, telling Sammy how he was growing into a fine young man. This was a man adored by his wife and children.

What had happened to Darryl? In his twenties he collided unexpectedly with something called grace. The unconditional love of a very different Father finally got through to him. He found acceptance in the beloved Son. God began speaking to him in a wonderful new language that penetrated his wounded soul.

So Darryl was passing on that language, the musical language of grace. He was giving his boy and girl a childhood immeasurably different from his own.

Darryl's transformation reminds me of what happened to Saul of Tarsus, an individual who couldn't tell an encouraging word from a club. This Pharisee of Pharisees began his career as a professional persecutor, one of those people who can't be happy unless they're making someone else miserable. But after Jesus stunned him on the road to Damascus and gave him a new name, Paul learned a radically new language. And he became a master encourager, the most beloved ambassador for Christ in the early church. You can see it in all his epistles. They all begin the same way—with a flood of gracious encouragement.

Do you find yourself looking for the right words? Ever wonder what you should say in a tough situation? The New Testament gives us a great Mustard Seed Secret: "Let your conversation be always full of grace, seasoned with salt, so that you may know how to answer everyone." To speak encouraging words, tap into grace. Grace gives you the right answer. That's a life-changing promise.

There's actually a point to the joke, "I wish people who have trouble communicating would just shut up." If you can't carry a tune, stop and listen. Listen to the great symphony of the Word made flesh, the Word rescuing the undeserving. Listen to God's terms of endearment that come through in the Epistles: children of God, beloved, the chosen, the anointed, vessels to be used for noble purposes, temples of the Holy Spirit, trophies led by Christ in triumphal procession.

Have you really savored these nicknames? They're not just theological categories to be dissected. They are precious notes that form a wonderful song.

Listen to grace. Become fluent in its musical language. It's the most powerful music there is. It's how we "speak to one another with psalms, hymns and spiritual songs." It's how we put a song in other people's hearts.

So let's look at a few important lyrics. Here's something grace typically says: "I believe in you." That line is really a matter of passing on to others the faith God has in us. If God can look through our sinfulness and see citizens of the kingdom, then we can adopt the same perspective. We can afford to affirm.

What kind of people did Jesus believe in? Well, there was Simon the Zealot, member of a violent political group. There was Matthew, who'd been collecting taxes from his own people for their hated Roman oppressors. Thomas was plagued with doubts. James and John had such violent tempers they were called "sons of thunder." And their leader, Simon Peter, rarely got his foot out of his mouth.

What was Jesus supposed to do with this motley crew? In spite of their shortcomings, he expressed great faith in them: "You'll become fishers of men." And they ended up making a fishing pond of the whole world.

Saying "I believe in you" is the opposite of judging. That's one thing Jesus warned us about very pointedly. To judge our neighbor is to stand back and issue a verdict. It's to scrunch up our faces as we're trying to look around the log in our eye to get at the speck in the other guy's.

The New Testament gives us no ground on which to separate ourselves. We're involved with the weakest among us. As Paul said, "You are in our hearts to die together and to live together." We have to believe in each other. We share in the same grace. We are justified by the same God. We're listening to the same music.

To judge our neighbor is to play the music backward. It's a garbled attempt to justify ourselves. Instead, celebrate God declaring you righteous by believing in the potential of others.

Judging points a finger. Grace gets its hands dirty.

Judging raises an eyebrow. Grace raises expectations.

Judging identifies wrongdoing. Grace identifies with wrongdoers.

Judging assumes, "You owe me." Grace proclaims, "Our debt is paid."

Judging writes off failures. Grace is written on tablets of human hearts.

Judging elbows others off the straight and narrow. Grace shows them the fast lane.

Judging shuts people out of the game. Grace is a talent scout.

Here's another great lyric in the music of grace: "You have a gift." The marvelous thing about belonging to Christ's body is that every single person, every single organism, has an irreplaceable role. From the hair follicles on our heads to the calluses on the balls of our feet, everything is vital. So we celebrate God gifting us by finding gifts in others. That's what grace looks for. It's in our power to help the gifts of others bloom.

Three students at a Michigan university began noticing a rather homely looking girl who always ate alone in the cafeteria. She was quiet—almost withdrawn—and didn't seem to have many friends on campus. The three men decided to try an experiment.

They began to talk to the girl around campus, sit with her at meals, and find out what she was really like. As the students shared their friendship, the girl seemed to blossom before their eyes. She revealed signs of a sparkling, witty personality. Her plainness gave way to hints of real beauty. One of the men was so impressed he eventually married her.

Grace calls us to lift people higher, spurring one another on toward love and good deeds, encouraging one another to lead a life worthy of God. Grace has to be spread around in order to remain potent. It doesn't increase when hoarded. It's a tune we pass along.

When we look for gifts in others, that process neutralizes our tendency to zero in on mistakes, to put adultery in headlines and an act of kindness in footnotes. We rush out and tell the world because we caught someone doing something right. Words of grace replace

the language of criticism because God's unconditional love has replaced insecurity.

The critical are always trying to straighten someone else out. Grace says, "He might have a great curveball."

The critical put people in their place. Grace takes people to the throne of mercy.

The critical snort at drawing outside the lines. Grace admires the colors.

The critical shoo a bunch of noisy, runny-nosed kids away. Grace says, "You have to become like them to enter my kingdom."

The critical identify themselves by who they're not. Grace has supper with publicans and prostitutes.

The critical take cheap (snap) shots. Grace makes a portrait of possibilities.

Intentionally building up other people saves us from a multitude of dysfunctional behaviors. That's the Mustard Seed Secret behind the command, "Encourage one another." We don't have to give our foul mood the pulpit. Wonderful things happen when grace takes the microphone.

In his letter, James tells us a lot about the power of this tiny organ, the tongue. It's the little rudder that steers the great ship. He warned that verbal sparks can set off a great conflagration. But the power of the tongue can be used for good as well. The musical language of grace can set off echoes felt around the world. It's a catchy song that every human heart recognizes, every human heart can learn.

In his late teens, my son Jason went through a skater-outlaw period that scared me quite a bit. He looked pretty hard-core with his orange hair, nipple rings, and trousers so baggy you could drive a pickup through the pant leg. He didn't seem remotely connected to anything related to God or the church.

But one dark night something happened that shot this "slacker kid" to the ceiling with excitement. Jason told me it was all he could do to keep from jumping up and down and yelling, "You the Man,

God. It's you and me. Where do you want me to go next? What's my next mission?"

It actually happened in a county jail cell. That's where I had to go pick him up one morning. It was one of those times when you wonder if you've completely blown it as a parent.

I cringed as he described rolling around golfing greens, flat on his skateboard, trying to flee police searchlights at 1 A.M. He and a buddy, just for a lark, had broken into a snack shack on the course. Eventually, as the older of the two, Jason was caught and detained.

But then my son told me about an encounter behind bars with another very troubled young man. Andrew's matted, greasy hair and dull gray eyes spoke of years in and out of jail. But as he talked about his troubles, insightful, intelligent phrases sometimes flashed through. Jason got the distinct impression this guy could have made something out of his life. But he just kept blowing it.

At one point Andrew rambled a bit about the possibility of "God having a plan for your life."

What hopeful words can there be for someone whose young life is going down the toilet? I don't know why Jason remembered the story of the footprints. But he said he really felt for this cellmate and began telling him about a man looking back over his life and seeing two sets of footprints traced along in the sand. You probably know this familiar story. The tracks are those of God walking beside an individual through his ups and downs. At the very lowest point, however, one set of the footprints disappears. The man asks in dismay, "God, why did you desert me?"

"I didn't desert you," God replies. "That's when I was carrying you."

After Jason finished the parable, Andrew's dull eyes lit up. Then, to my son's astonishment, he dropped from the iron bench to his knees and began praying out loud. He poured out his heart to God for twenty minutes, sobbing uncontrollably, forehead to the cold cement floor.

Guards took Andrew to another cell and ushered in a new prisoner, who asked, "What happened to him?"

Jason, still in awe, could only reply, "He found God."

"That's cool."

And that's when Jason almost hit the ceiling with a new sense of mission—a rendezvous at a point of need, like mine with Peggy in Japan long ago. Seconds later he was reminded, "Well, don't get too uppity; you've been screwing up too."

"Yeah, you're right. You're the Man."

What Jason had run into, face to face, was the awesome power of encouraging words. It swept him up in a kind of exhilaration he'd never felt before.

"I believe in you." "You have a gift." You can share grace in many different ways. What matters is that you're passing on God's great musical language.

Cited:

Encourage, build up—Hebrews 3:13; 1 Thessalonians 5:11;
    1 Thessalonians 4:18
Conversation full of grace—Colossians 4:6
Spiritual songs—Ephesians 5:19
Fishers of men—Matthew 4:19
Live and die together—2 Corinthians 7:3, NASB
Spurring one another on—Hebrews 10:24
Lives worthy of God—1 Thessalonians 2:12

CHAPTER SIX

Sustain JOY

Create contentment through the leverage of praise

IN ONE of my few attempts to be a real Harry Homeowner, I carpeted the garage and turned it into a playroom for the kids. Unfortunately, our house backed up against a steep hill, and during heavy rains, water would wash through the back door and flood the garage floor.

After drying out the carpet several times, I decided to fix the problem once and for all. I built a low, cinder-block wall around the back door to divert the water. Then I put up a sheet of corrugated plastic roofing above the door to keep rain from collecting there in the entryway.

I was pretty proud of my handiwork. No matter how hard it rained now, water wasn't going to flood my garage.

Two days after I'd completed that project, our washing machine in the garage went berserk during the spin cycle. A hose shook loose and shot water everywhere—completely soaking the carpet.

Even when it doesn't rain, it pours. Ever feel you just can't win? Sometimes it seems misfortune doesn't just strike at random, it conspires against you. And it's natural to think, "Sure, I could be happy if only . . ."

If only for the wrong circumstances. They keep throwing a wrench in our well-laid plans. Everything will be great as soon as this debt is paid off, or as soon as my neighbor moves away, or as soon as I get a promotion.

But the truth is, human happiness isn't very sustainable, even in the right circumstances, even in paradise. When things get tough at the office, many of us dream of an idyllic vacation in the South Pacific. But on the islands of Micronesia, where we picture carefree, barefoot people fishing and playing all day, the number-one cause of death is . . . suicide. It's become an epidemic among young men: the rate for them is twenty times higher than in the United States.

Recently researchers have documented the fact that happiness doesn't last long even when your wildest financial dreams come true. David Myers, author of *The Pursuit of Happiness,* reports, "Even people who have won a state lottery or a British pool gain only a temporary jolt of joy." A year later they are only slightly happier than before the windfall. University of London psychologist Michael Eysenck explains: "Major events lose their impact over time. You adjust your lifestyle and your expectations."

In other words, millionaires soon settle down to dreading one day at a time—just like other people. We just don't sustain joy very well.

But guess what? The New Testament isn't intimidated by all this. Against the glum backdrop of human nature, it's constantly spray-painting joyful slogans in the wildest colors: Fifty-nine references to joy. Eighty-one instances of "rejoice." That's a lot of graffiti. And what all this advertises is a joy that lasts, happiness that's sustainable—even for mere mortals.

Jesus spoke of an inner spring that could well up to life everlasting. Paul wrote of a joy that "knows no bounds" and commended joy overflowing in "the most severe trial."

New Testament joy isn't just something that drops by unexpectedly and can't stay for supper. It actually fills human beings. Peter maintained that believers can be "filled with an inexpressible and glorious joy."

Who wouldn't want that? How many lottery tickets and island vacations would you go through for that?

The New Testament does in fact show us the secret of sustainable joy. It's found in one of the precepts it emphasizes the most. Paul gives us this Mustard Seed Secret in Philippians: "Rejoice in the Lord always; again I will say, rejoice!" New Testament joy is focused on God, on his character, on the hope of being with him in the future, on the assurance of his presence today.

We can rejoice always when we rejoice in the Lord. That's a life-changing promise. It's a simple principle that solves one of the great human dilemmas. Joy is one of the things we want the most. But oddly, we can't get it by pursuing it directly. If we just grab for the gusto, it slips through our fingers. After we've gobbled up the chocolate cake, we get sick just looking at bits of icing on the plate.

Happiness is a by-product. We get it by aiming somewhere else. That's why this Mustard Seed Secret is so powerful. It shows us the best place to aim. After all, God isn't here today and gone tomorrow. He doesn't get up on the wrong side of the bed. His love and grace and nurture don't shut down for repairs. We can rejoice always when we rejoice in the God whose eternal qualities are on display 24/7.

But how exactly do we do that? How do we accomplish that in the real world? Our path through life isn't bordered by stained-glass windows. It's pocketed with neighbor kids who break windows and coworkers who talk behind our backs to the boss. It's haunted by laptops that drive us crazy because we've just spent four hours on the phone with a Microsoft tech and we still can't get our e-mail. It's filled with clogged freeways, high-maintenance conveniences, numbing television, stressful vacations, and adult children of alcoholics. How do we rejoice in the Lord when so many things are pressing us down?

Some years ago the whole world seemed to be pressing down on me in the wake of a divorce. I was stubbornly resisting "recovery." It was easier to blame people and complain to God: Why did you let this happen to me? I sought your guidance so prayerfully and carefully. Why didn't you prevent this disaster?

I'd become painfully aware that I'd let a destructive situation go on far too long. The big failure made me wonder if I hadn't made stupid choices all my life. I rehearsed all the nasty things I was never, never going to let happen to me again. "God's wonderful plan" sometimes seemed as outdated and distant as a dirigible.

One morning in January I crawled out of bed, slipped into my car, and headed south on the Ventura freeway. The sun shone brightly over hills bursting with greenery. That happens for about fifteen minutes in dry Southern California, after the winter rains. As I drove by swaying oak trees near Agoura, I suddenly felt compelled to do something I hadn't in some time: praise God. I was still feeling resentful and rebellious. But why not give it a shot?

Passing Malibu Canyon Road I acknowledged that God was still exalted in the heavens even if I might be stuck in the dumps. I spoke to him about his acts of compassion new every morning, his strong right hand eager to rescue, his patience with the stubborn and stiff-necked. And those compliments I was sending heavenward started grabbing hold of me. Okay, God's pretty amazing.

I felt it, even through the San Fernando Valley filled with aging condos and tacky strip malls. The God who visits the earth and causes it to overflow is worthy of my worship. As I praised God for more and more things, I began to remember more and more things to praise him for. God had visited my life. Yes, there were those incredible times with Campus Crusade at Western Illinois University. And yes, the most precious friendships, the most stimulating relationships, had this Lord at the center. I remembered teaching Bible at the English School in Japan and how exciting it was to see the light come on in students' eyes.

I kept praising through Van Nuys, Burbank, Pasadena. Driving in smoggy LA isn't the most inspirational experience in the world, but I was actually enjoying God's company. His blessings had begun to sink in. They began to weigh on my heart and make room for the height and depth and breadth of the love of Christ.

I couldn't stop celebrating him. Ugly landfills, gaudy billboards, and gray buildings whizzed by, but I was still in the green hills with the psalmist.

And right there in the middle of the eastbound 210, something bowled me over. This is why my life has been so good. It's all tied to God. He's behind all the great moments. The greatest joy and peace I've felt have come when I've caught a glimpse of his goodness.

I'd been looking back at negative stuff for so long. I'd allowed a broken marriage to discolor everything that went before. I'd seen only the betrayal, and not my part in it. I'd ached and anguished because there seemed to be no plan I could fit into.

But during that drive I suddenly found the Big Picture. Praise had opened it up. I wasn't groping around for it anymore; I was in it. My life was part of a plan that stretched from horizon to horizon. God redeemed my failures and struggles and gave meaning to them.

That's the day that five years of rebellion and anger began to melt away. I was blinking back tears, trying to stay in my lane so the semi trucks roaring by wouldn't run over me. But the eyes of my heart were opened. I knew beyond a doubt what a blessing God had been in my life. I could have honked my horn all the way to San Bernardino out of pure joy.

Developing a habit of praise is the most practical way we can rejoice in the Lord.

The New Testament urges us to make this a continual part of our lives: "Through Jesus, therefore, let us continually offer to God a sacrifice of praise—the fruit of lips that confess his name."

Part of the great Mustard Seed Secret about rejoicing in the Lord always is that we rejoice in the bad times—when the washer hose shakes loose. In fact, that's when praise works most powerfully. It's very similar to the dynamic of thankfulness.

The Greek mathematician Archimedes shocked people into seeing the power of leverage by boasting that he could lift the whole world—with a long enough lever. It's all about counterweight, using an object pressing down on a lever to lift an object on the other side of the fulcrum.

God is the ultimate Man of Substance in the universe. He can serve as counterweight to any kind of misfortune that presses down on us. But in order to do that he can't just be an abstraction in the distance. He can't just be a vague figure we call for in emergencies. He has to have presence; he has to have weight. And it's the praise that gives him weight: God inhabits the praises of his people. Praise fills in the picture. It illuminates his wonderful qualities. It makes him a specific Person in our world.

The more heartfelt our praises, the more of a counterweight God becomes. Yes, what happened to me was bad, but look at how gracious God is. Yes, that was a painful loss, but look at how God works good out of evil.

Praise gives us great leverage. Burdens become much more manageable and movable because God is big enough to counterbalance any kind of calamity.

Let me expand on this idea of leverage with something the apostle Peter wrote: "Rejoice that you participate in the sufferings of Christ, so that you may be overjoyed when his glory is revealed." Peter was writing to believers who were going through hard times because of hostile Roman authorities. The skies weren't blue and the robins weren't chirping. But he asked his readers to focus on the fact that it's honorable to suffer for the sake of Christ. And he said that if they rejoice in the bad times, they'll be overjoyed later, when Christ appears gloriously.

There's a wonderful principle here. People who praise God in misfortune are exercising their spirits. They're resisting the pressure

to give in to self-pity and despair. They're becoming more buoyant. They're using the leverage of praise to lift heavy burdens.

So what happens when things are light and sunny? They shoot upward. They're "overjoyed." It's like a person who's beefed up after working with weights. When he goes back to the lighter weights he started with, they feel like nothing at all.

People who just whine during the bad times don't get any exercise in weight lifting. As a result, they find something to whine about during the good times too. They lose their capacity to be overjoyed.

One of the most joyful people I've ever met is a Cuban pastor named Humberto Noble Alexander. He's one of those individuals who always has a sparkle in his eyes, like he's just been let in on a wonderful secret. Humberto has been through hard times financially since coming to the States, but nothing seems to get him down.

This man spent the best years of his life in one of Castro's prisons for the politically incorrect. He endured brutal attempts at "reeducation" for two decades, but he refused to bend to Communist ideology.

Instead he led clandestine worship services in the prison. His joyful faith was so contagious that many fellow inmates wanted to commit their lives to the Christ. Humberto couldn't stop praising. In fact, this cheery man baptized two hundred of them — right under the noses of the guards!

I couldn't imagine how this had happened. Humberto barely managed to keep a small Bible concealed from prying eyes as he passed it from one interested inmate to another. He explained he usually pulled baptisms off during the noon meal. Each cell block of men entered and left the mess hall at a certain time. One group would file in past a long trough of water where they washed up, while another group filed out on the other side.

On the appointed day, Humberto would make sure he sneaked into the group going out, as the man to be baptized was going in. Usually that meant skipping a meal. As the two lines approached the trough, the men slowed their pace and bunched together tightly.

The candidate slipped into the water. Pastor Humberto immersed him in the name of the Father, Son, and Holy Spirit. Then they'd slip back in line and proceed on their way.

As Humberto was telling me this, I kept waiting for the punch line. I could picture the baptized inmate walking around, dripping wet, making puddles in the mess hall. Pastor Humberto's uniform is wet too. How do they keep prison officials from finding out? How do they avoid the inevitable punishment?

The punch line didn't come, and I asked, "But didn't the authorities find out you immersed someone again?"

Humberto replied, "Oh, sure, they usually did." And then he grinned at me and said, "But he'd already been baptized."

Would Pastor Humberto be beaten? Yes, probably. Would he be thrown into solitary? Yes, most likely. But what mattered, what he praised God about, was that a new individual had started a spiritual journey.

Humberto Noble Alexander learned to rejoice then, under the worst of circumstances. He is overjoyed now, in a place of freedom.

With the leverage of praise, we will always travel light.

Cited:

Happiness studies—*Christianity Today,* November 23, 1992, page 24

Well up—John 4

No bounds—2 Corinthians 7:4

Overflowing—2 Corinthians 8:2

Inexpressible—1 Peter 1:8

Rejoice always—Philippians 4:4, NASB

Sacrifice of praise—Hebrews 13:15

God inhabits praises—Psalm 22:3, KJV

Overjoyed—1 Peter 4:13

Persist PATIENTLY

Avoid burnout by finding something to express

WHEN THERE were no ditches to dig or hedges to trim or walls to paint, the boys could always be sent out after the weeds. That was the job waiting for us at the Christian academy where I spent my high school years. So we'd straggle out over the campus lawns with that looping shuffle of paid-by-the-hour peons, dragging our hoes behind us. My buddy Arnold and I would wander over and check out a few dandelions, ponder their relative merits, and then begin bothering one to death. There wasn't any realistic hope of getting all the weeds; our school included several wide fields. We were just putting in time — watching a beautiful Sunday afternoon go by — hack, hack, hack.

One of the reasons I can't forget those hours is that they became in my mind a picture of religious life. What do Christians *do* anyway? They hoe weeds. At least that's what it seemed to most of us at the academy — restless teenagers on a twenty-four-hour-a-day call to rectitude. You have to keep fighting off the evils of the world that creep up around you. *Look out, there's a patch of lust springing up over there—you know how fast that stuff grows. Wow, here's a string of Satanism subtly infiltrating the church. And, oh, right under your feet, a thorny cluster of doctrinal error. Better get that.*

That was our image of religious goodness. Hacking at weeds. I mean, you can't just let sin take over your life, right? You have to keep at it. The dark, fertile soil of human nature is always threatening, always sprouting up dandelions.

And that's the problem. You never really have any hope of getting it all. You no sooner hack away at one thing than something else is growing like crazy somewhere else. And so a lot of people burn out. They just get tired of hoeing weeds. Why not roll around in them for a while?

Many of my peers burned out on being good; they gave up. I am still haunted by their faces in the yearbook.

The New Testament takes very seriously our human tendency to grow weary in the "good fight of the faith." One of the things it urges us to do over and over is persist patiently, endure, persevere, stand firm. It spotlights these qualities more than seventy times.

The author of Hebrews frequently reminded his readers of the need to persevere in order to receive what was promised. Paul urged the Thessalonians to "never tire of doing what is right," the Galatians to "not become weary in doing good," and the Romans to remember "persistence in doing good." Peter included perseverance in his list of Christian virtues that we are to possess "in increasing measure." James wrote that "perseverance must finish its work so that you may be mature and complete."

But the question is, of course, How are we to fulfill these essential New Testament precepts without burning out on being good? Is there an alternative to a lifetime of hoeing weeds?

I believe the author of Hebrews gave us a fantastic Mustard Seed Secret: "Let us run with perseverance the race marked out for us. Let us fix our eyes on Jesus, the author and perfecter of our faith." There's a life-changing promise in this little bit of Scripture. Hebrews is giving us an answer for burnout. It's showing us that we can run with perseverance when we run with our eyes fixed on Jesus. But here's the key: this fixed gaze isn't just a grim determination to follow the example of the perfect Master. It's about having an object of inspiration. It's about having something to express. That's what Paul was after when he prayed that believers would be given "the Spirit of wisdom and revelation" to enlighten the eyes of the heart so we could grasp the "glorious inheritance" and the "incomparably great power" and the "fullness" of Jesus Christ.

In thinking about how we can persist in the spiritual life, I have been struck by the way artists pursue their craft. What drives them, year after year? Why do they often endure years of privation and loneliness as they work away on that novel or those paintings?

Think of painters staring at the same things we all do. What drove Claude Monet to keep doing canvases of the same old water lilies? What drove Vincent Van Gogh to keep painting those same wheat fields?

Great painters simply look until they find something to admire. They look carefully; they involve their intellect and emotions—and then something hits them. They see something achingly beautiful in a line of trees against the clouds. They see something strikingly true in the lines on a grandmother's face.

Now they have something to express, something to say through their canvases. And they will spend hour after hour, day after day, working happily until they've given shape and color to the thing they admire.

You'll find tremendous energy for your spiritual life when you look at Jesus—with the eyes of an artist. Don't just paint by the numbers. Don't just see a list of duties in Christ's perfect life that you have to try to reproduce. Look at his life in the Word until you find something you can personally admire, something beautiful and true that strikes you. And then find some way to express it in your life.

Imagine two painters standing side by side in a field. Both are wielding brushes. Both are covering a surface with paint. The arms of both get tired.

Mary, however, is covering a wall with whitewash. Like the weed-hoers back at the academy, she's paid by the hour.

Bill is staring off at a willow drooping over a pond. He's trying to capture something in this landscape on a canvas.

Both painters are going through very similar motions. But they're in two completely different worlds. Mary is glancing at her watch, waiting for the next coffee break, eager for 5 P.M. The afternoon drags on. Bill, on the other hand, is caught up in his task; the only thing that can drive him away is darkness.

The essential difference between the painter and . . . the painter is that one has something to express, the other doesn't. Two believers can go through very similar motions—engage in similar acts of worship and charity—and yet inhabit completely different worlds. One is covering a wall with whitewash—uninspired, performing Christian duties. The other is expressing something great about the God he admires.

It's just a mustard-seed step. It's just a matter of looking until you can admire and admiring until you have something to express. But it can give your spiritual life legs for the long run.

Ever get tired of changing diapers? I reached that point pretty quickly when my son was a baby. In those days we were trying to be frugal and "natural," and we used cloth diapers that had to be washed out in the toilet. Not something you want to make a career of.

But one evening as I was bent over the bowl, trying to hold my nose and rinsing out an awful mess, I saw something to admire. What did Jesus actually do in that Upper Room when he washed his disciples' feet before the Last Supper? We usually idealize the scenes in rosy candlelight, with Bach playing in the background. But those were some nasty feet that had been trudging in sandals over

Jerusalem's muddy cobblestones. Jesus had become a servant in the details, with a towel over his knee and his hands in a basin filled with soiled water. That's how he expressed his love.

It struck me pretty hard there in the bathroom. And it turned my little chore into something of a sacrament. This was one very specific way I could express my love for my infant son.

Having something to express gave me legs when it came to diaper duty.

We run best by fixing the eyes of our hearts on Jesus. We run best when we have something we want to say about God. If you don't have that momentum, guess what your life will center on? Sin. It's not that you're indulging all the time. It's that you're pointing it out, glaring at it, shaking a finger at it, trying to shun it. You start identifying yourself by what you avoid: I don't drink; I don't dance; I don't play around. Sin remains the center of attention.

If you don't have something great you want to express about God, you'll always fall back on hoeing weeds. It's not "persistence in doing good" that burns people out. It's the religion of avoidance. Always having to be on guard, always having to say no, is simply not sustainable.

If I have nothing to say about God in church, I'll probably be complaining about those boring nineteenth-century hymns. But if I want to express something, I can do it through quaint lyrics about "billows of love" and "hearts with rapture thrilled."

If I have nothing to admire about God in prayer, it becomes an exercise in concentration. If I do, prayer becomes a window on God's face.

If I have nothing to say about God, my neighbor telling me his car broke down is just another obligation. If I'm inspired, it's an opportunity to express God's generosity.

Jesus once said, "The kingdom of heaven is like treasure hidden in a field. When a man found it, he hid it again, and then in his joy went out and sold all he had and bought that field." Here we have a man getting rid of all his worldly possessions. Why? In order to avoid the love of money? In order to make a big sacrifice? No, he wanted to get hold of this hidden treasure, and it was worth selling out for. In his joy he went out and sold all he had.

We run with perseverance when we're in hot pursuit. We successfully get rid of the bad by pursuing something better. We're running after love, peace, and grace, so we get rid of stuff that gets in the way. We "throw off" the sin "that so easily entangles" by fixing our gaze on the "author and perfecter of our faith."

Don't just flail against your bad temper. Aim at being more malleable. Express the divine forbearance that shows mercy to the worst of sinners.

Don't just stare down lust. Seek to develop sensitivity. Express the way Jesus touched people's hearts with surgical precision.

Don't just stamp out resentment. Pursue compassion. Say something about the way God reaches out to those who wrong him.

Don't just fight depression. Practice thankfulness—ahead of time. Talk about the blessings that are still disguised as mishaps.

Because of who God is, our pursuit of these qualities is tied to something profound. Every righteous act is like a dab of paint on a great canvas; it adds to the glory of God; it fills out the picture. God doesn't want our religion to shrink into a matter of putting square pegs in square holes. He wants to expand our lives with his positive qualities. Fill your minds, Paul said, with "whatever is true, whatever is noble . . . whatever is admirable—if anything is excellent or praiseworthy—think about such things." Goodness isn't a matter of cutting life down to proper size; it's a matter of growing into "the whole measure of the fullness of Christ." It's about creating something beautiful for God. So start looking with the eyes of an artist. Start looking for things to admire, things you want to express. Inspiration is out there in the most unexpected places.

I remember a day in my early twenties when I was slouched in a back pew after a worship service, wondering, as usual, why church had to be so boring. The feeble organ music had finally trickled away altogether. Why did the religious life seem to attract mainly the old—those who didn't seem to have the energy to sin? I was casting a disapproving eye on the smattering of old women in the church who, I imagined, had nothing better to do than warble these tired hymns all day. They were all sitting down one side of the center aisle, no doubt so they could slip quickly to the lobby afterward and start gossiping, I thought.

There was one blind man sitting alone near the front of the church who lingered in the silence too. No one had sat in his pew. There, I thought, was someone as isolated as myself. Nothing in the service seemed to have touched him either.

This stranger finally rose from his pew, fumbled for a huge book, thick with Braille, and slipped it under his arm. He was a stocky gentleman who moved rather clumsily. Turning uncertainly, he began to make his way toward the rear of the sanctuary.

Immediately, the old woman just behind him reached out and clasped his hands tightly. They exchanged a few animated words. He stepped forward and the next woman at the aisle reached for his hands in greeting, then the next. Each woman beamed as she said his name and expressed her delight in seeing him.

I realized that, in this way, the women had formed an unobtrusive escort, passing him from hand to hand, guiding his steps to the foyer. He wasn't just led, like some lost child. He was carried along like a celebrity. As he came closer, the man's face transfixed me. Around those sunken, glazed eyes, his features shouted joy. Even I could see that the feeble, wrinkled hands of the women had really touched him.

I'd been sitting there identifying myself by what I excluded, by what I was not. They were showing me what God is like. Those old women, as a tag team, were still running strong in the race. They had something to say, something wonderful to express about the God who leads us "with cords of human kindness, with ties of love."

Cited:

Fight the good fight—1 Timothy 6:12
Receiving what's promised—Hebrews 10:36
Never tire—2 Thessalonians 3:13
Not weary—Galatians 6:9
Doing good—Romans 2:7
Increasing measure—2 Peter 1:6-8
Finish its work—James 1:4
The race—Hebrews 12:1-2
Spirit of wisdom—Ephesians 1:17-23
Treasure hidden—Matthew 13:44
Pursue love, peace—2 Timothy 2:22
Throw off sin—Hebrews 12:1-2
Fill your minds—Philippians 4:8
The whole measure—Ephesians 4:13
Cords of kindness—Hosea 11:4

CHAPTER EIGHT

CHEERFULLY

Enlarge your capacity to receive by opening your hand

WHEN THE aliens were about to come for my grandmother, the first thing she thought about was her hair. It was a mess and they'd be here any minute. She was sitting on the side of her bed at one in the morning, with the unearthly rumbling that had awakened her still ringing in her ears. And out her window the dark sky had lit up with an eerie green glow.

It had to be an E.T. invasion of some kind and the oddest thing was that, in her groggy shock, Grandmother could only think about being presentable. People were coming to her home, the comfortable, two-story river flat Grandad had built near the Gulf for their retirement. What would they think of her living-room furniture? What would they think of the way she was dressed? Grandmother glanced in the floor-length mirror and smoothed her wrinkled nightgown. Did she have time to get ready? The sky was changing from an eerie green to an even stranger purple.

As it turned out, the Martians made no house calls that night. The following day Grandmother learned there had been an explosion at a natural gas plant nearby. But it had sure seemed to her like a cosmic "Guess who's coming to dinner."

Isn't it funny, the things we worry about in moments of crisis. It's like Mom telling you to always wear clean underwear in case you're in a car accident. But our "trivial" concerns sometimes expose deeper ones. Near the heart of all human endeavor is a desire to be presentable, to be accepted, to be affirmed in our own homes.

We want to feel secure. And it's easy to subconsciously depend on accessories for that security—the old story of relying on the size of our house or the speed of our computer or the brand of our outfit to feel good about ourselves. At times we get caught up in the pursuit of material things as a substitute for filling the holes in our lives. We half believe that a new set of dishware will cure our irritability. We sort of hope the new big-screen TV will bring us closer as a family.

Nice things sometimes help. But trying to build security by accumulating possessions is like getting ready for the end times by putting on more makeup—it's the Second Coming and I don't have a thing to wear!

Greed is a dead end. That's why Jesus warned us so strongly about the love of money and Paul wrote about the danger of placing our hope in wealth. Financial security is an oxymoron. We can never get enough to feel secure.

So how do we gain lasting security? Jesus gives us a wonderful Mustard Seed Secret that shows us the absolute best way to feel secure. This promise is dynamite: "Give, and it will be given to you; good measure, pressed down, shaken together, running over, they will pour into your lap. For by your standard of measure it will be measured to you in return."

Generosity changes the world. That's why it's one of the qualities most emphasized in the New Testament. It changes the world in extraordinary ways. What was once a stingy, barren landscape can be

transformed into a place of abundance—overflowing onto our laps. Giving is the best way to get enough.

And there's a very important reason why this is true. Giving enlarges our capacity to receive. It affects the state of our hearts. Jesus urged his followers to lay up treasures in heaven: "For where your treasure is, there your heart will be also." When we lift up our resources to heaven, our hearts are lifted up to heaven. When we enlarge our giving, our hearts are enlarged.

It's human nature to cling tightly to "visible means of support." It's human nature to grab more in order to feel safer. But the New Testament encourages the opposite impulse. When we open our hands, when we express generosity in some way, something happens to our grasp. We are able to take in "good measure, pressed down, shaken together."

Countless people have found this true when it comes to cold, hard cash. You may have heard the dramatic examples: Colgate and Penney determined to return a faithful tithe to the Lord no matter what—and went on to build world-class companies. And there are the smaller stories, a single mother who gives back to God out of her meager means, runs out of diapers one day, prays earnestly, and watches a stranger walk up to her and deposit a huge bundle of Huggies in her lap.

But the same principle applies when it comes to time. In our middle-age years, many of us get pretty stingy with this commodity. It doesn't stretch ahead indefinitely. We resent people who take up our time without good reason. Don't call. Don't write. Don't knock on my door. I'll contact you.

That happened to me after I found myself suddenly single in midlife. I got to the point where I was trying to remove all the hassles from my life. I wanted a vehicle that never needed repairs. I wanted a yard that mowed itself. I didn't want any people around who gave me chores.

Finally, by whittling my day-to-day down to the essentials, I managed to hoard some real quality time for myself. What did I do with it? I played solitaire every night while watching old movies on TV.

Then I got to know a woman at church who was struggling to raise three little boys by herself. My kids were in college. Been there, done that. But she was such an intriguing person I took them all out to lunch sometimes after services. And one night I found myself playing hide-and-seek in the dark with the boys. A couple of hours flew by. I'd missed another Humphrey Bogart adventure. But the laughter of those kids filled me up in a way nothing had for a long, long time.

I didn't really find "quality time" until I gave a little of it away.

The same principle applies when it comes to our homes. If we've finally managed to mortgage our way into a dream house, we get pretty particular about who we let inside. We don't want to wear out the carpet. We don't want the bratty neighborhood kids bumping over the lamps.

And of course it's natural for our circle of friends to slowly constrict around the people who go with our nice furniture. Jesus had another suggestion: "When you give a banquet, invite the poor, the crippled, the lame, the blind, and you will be blessed."

After my kids began living near their college, I presided over an orderly, nicely decorated house that only a few selected buddies ever visited. They cleaned up after themselves.

But then one day people outside my circle tramped into my sanctuary. It happened only because I was shooting a few scenes for a television series at my house. They changed their clothes in the bedrooms; they practiced lines in the hallways; they rearranged the living room; they ate lunch all over the place and left a big mess behind.

But afterward, in the stillness of the evening, what I remembered were the voices and how they warmed me. I didn't really find my home until I opened it up to strangers and they filled it up with their very different stories from very different backgrounds. My house had become terribly vacant without hospitality.

It's natural to try to build security by filling our homes with wonderful things and keeping them nice. But the more we concentrate on these accessories, the emptier our lives become. Our security seeps out the back door. And we keep buying new stuff to replace it.

The only way to shut the back door is to open the front door. When we open it a little wider, we'll find we can receive full measure, pressed down and running over.

The New Testament points out that a particular kind of giving enlarges our capacity to receive. Paul summed it up perfectly: "God loves a cheerful giver." Some give grimly, to fulfill an obligation. Some give little, because their heart isn't in it. But to give cheerfully is to give because God has been generous to you. God loves a cheerful giver. And a cheerful giver is conscious of God's love. You trust that you'll be okay if you give; you'll be provided for.

It's an ever-expanding circle. Being conscious of God's love makes you more generous. And being generous makes you more conscious of God's love. But this isn't a closed circle; you can enter at any point. Any little steps we take in this process help us to get into the wonderfully self-reinforcing circle of generosity and love. We can claim a promise: "You will be made rich in every way so that you can be generous on every occasion."

Jesus spotlighted the widow at the temple who gave two mites as an example of giving that changes the world. Her tiny gift, he said, outweighed all the gold coins clattering into the coffer from the wealthy donors. Why? Because her heart was in her giving. She gave everything. And that wonderfully enlarged her capacity to receive.

As Paul pointed out, even extreme poverty can well up in rich generosity.

People who picture giving as a means to become wealthy miss the point. As Jesus reminds us, life doesn't consist in the abundance of our possessions. Robert Graves once wrote, "There is no money in poetry, but then there is no poetry in money, either." We aren't enriched simply by having a lot of things. That generally dulls us. We are enriched by becoming more sensitive to beauty, more appreciative of blessings, more open to friendships, more responsive to insights.

Cheerful giving opens us up. That's a great Mustard Seed Secret. What makes the difference between happiness and misery in life? Much of the answer depends on whether our hearts are shrinking or stretching.

Instead of shrinking nervously around your rigid financial plan for the future, you give God a little room to work.

Instead of shrinking angrily around your "unmet needs," you give a friend a little support.

Instead of shrinking tightly around some recognition that comes your way, you give someone else a little credit.

Instead of shrinking around some possible slight, you give someone the benefit of the doubt.

Instead of shrinking around godliness as "a means to financial gain," you trust in the God who "richly provides us with everything for our enjoyment."

Cheerful giving, not conspicuous consumption, creates the good life. The Christ who promised us life in all its abundance is the Christ who calls us to radical giving.

Why go a second mile with the one who demands you walk one? Because it enlarges your capacity to receive.

Why give your cloak to the one who takes your tunic? Because it enlarges your capacity to receive.

Why did Jesus ask the rich young ruler to liquidate all his assets and give to the poor? Because the ruler's shrunken heart needed to be shaken loose so it could absorb the good life.

I experienced a bit of shaking during a night vigil at McDonough County Hospital. My two brothers and I had been working by Dad's bedside through the day, trying to keep him suctioned. We'd push his restless tongue flat with a suppressor, as the nurses had shown us, and wiggle a tube gingerly down his throat, hoping to

keep the congestion from turning into full-blown pneumonia.

Dan, Jerry, and I had flown to Illinois after we got news of the massive stroke. I had come with anxious expectations. I didn't want to see those familiar ruddy features wasting away. But it wasn't his face, still holding a bit of color, that shocked me. It was his terrible struggle for breath, chest and abdomen heaving, eyes rolling, never a moment's rest. I wasn't ready for suffering. Dad's limbs were weak, his moans strong. If only he could get a little rest.

My father was a man of few fears. We boys grew up under the umbrella of his steadfast moral courage. But he had expressed one apprehension: he didn't want to die in a hospital—life taken away in small clinical pieces.

That night the three of us stayed awake in Room 311, watching over the helpless man who had changed our diapers. We switched his position at regular intervals, fiddled with the blankets, and jumped up whenever he groaned.

Something happened to me during those long, dark hours. It came in the pungent smell of hay. That afternoon I'd rushed to the house to get a bite to eat and had taken a peek inside the barn Dad had built for his horses. He'd put up most of it by himself. Every oak beam was as sturdy as ever. Dad built well.

I remembered all the times I'd relied on him. I was five and slipped off his back while he was climbing out of the swimming pool. I couldn't swim, but they say I just calmly sank deeper under water, sure that Dad would fetch me out again. And of course he did.

I was twelve, walking with him in the woods he loved. It was always easy to talk. I had so many questions about right and wrong. And he lived the answers.

I was twenty, coming home from college on vacation. We would sit out on the porch looking at the sunset. When I shared how my faith was growing, his eyes would sparkle.

At 2 A.M. in that hospital room, these things became much more than memories. Slowly I began to understand why Dad always got up in the middle of the night to check on us and smooth our blankets—even after we were older. This was the only time I had waited up for the one who was up so many nights for me.

It was unexplored territory, and in its strange stillness I came face to face with the power of his love for me. It was as vivid as the wide Midwestern sky dancing with stars just outside the window. At that moment I knew beyond a doubt I would love my children with the same unquenchable desire.

About ten the next morning, my brothers and I returned to the hospital after a couple hours of sleep. Nurses had disconnected the oxygen. Dad was breathing just fine on his own. They said they thought he'd licked the pneumonia. One said, "A miracle is just what we needed around here."

Yes, the clearing of Dad's lungs, the widening of my heart—I could hardly contain the stuff of miracles.

Cited:

Full measure—Luke 6:38, NASB
Treasures in heaven—Matthew 6:21
Invite the poor—Luke 14:13-14
Cheerful giver—2 Corinthians 9:7
Generous on every occasion—2 Corinthians 9:11
Widow's mite—Mark 12:41-44
Extreme poverty—2 Corinthians 8:2
Abundance of possessions—Luke 12:15
Godliness and gain—1 Timothy 6:5
Richly provides—1 Timothy 6:17
Second mile—Matthew 5:41
Give your tunic—Matthew 5:40
Rich young ruler—Mark 10:17-21

Spread PEACE

Disarm "difficult people" by spotting their needs

WHEN JOSEPH was ordered by a court to divide all his property equally with his ex-wife, he grabbed a chain saw and cut their tri-level ranch house precisely in half.

When Judy got tired of her professor boyfriend working late on his pet project, she lit a match to the stack of folders on his desk— consuming a decade of effort on a new dictionary.

When Sam kept putting dimes in the parking meter and it still registered "No Time Remaining," he tore it up from the sidewalk and stomped down to the police station to show them it didn't work.

"Difficult people." We're going to run into them at some point in our lives. It may be someone road raging on the freeway. It may be a manipulative boss at the office. It may be a supposedly born-again individual at church who's an even bigger pain the second time around. We may get stuck in a relationship with a difficult person that's hard to end. In the worst of cases, these people can dominate our lives.

I remember interviewing the wife of a celebrity pastor who told me about an incident that happened right after her engagement. A shrewish acquaintance had taken her aside and, shaking a finger in her face, told her, "Your fiancé has a bright future; you make sure he finishes his education!" In other words: don't force him to leave school to support you.

As she told me this, I could see that the finger was still wagging in front of her face. That little incident occurred some forty years earlier, but she described it as indignantly as if it had happened yesterday.

Some difficult people are harder to shake than a pit bull with an ankle in its mouth. The problem is, the more we fight with them and the more we pray, "Lord, please don't let what that jerk did get me down," the deeper those teeth sink in. Difficult people can control us if we're attached in some way, if they can touch an old wound that hasn't quite been closed or if they hold the promise of meeting some unfulfilled need.

Difficult people out there are often a reflection of some difficulty in here. They mirror something we don't want to see. Have you ever caught yourself saying something like . . .

I just hate negative people!

You're always, always exaggerating!

You're being totally childish. So there.

Take back what you said about my impatience this very minute.

That male chauvinist pig is so insulting!

Of course he's a bigot. He's from Alabama.

It's absolutely impossible to be that sure about anything!

The compulsions in other people are so easy to pick out. Our own bad habits get pretty blurry. We may even find ourselves thinking in bumper-sticker terms: If you don't like my driving, get off the sidewalk.

In a world of difficult people, inside and out, the New Testament

offers us a rather startling promise. It's a promise implied in its many statements about living in peace—not just with our buddies, but with everyone.

In Romans we're asked to "live in harmony" and to "make every effort to do what leads to peace and to mutual edification." In Hebrews we're called to "live in peace with all men." Thessalonians repeats the call: "Live in peace with each other." Corinthians ups the ante with the hope that we "may be perfectly united in mind and thought." And Jesus asked the Father that his followers "may be one . . . just as you are in me and I am in you."

The early Christians were no strangers to difficult people. They had to survive the wrath of Jewish fanatics and the oppressive control of Rome. But the call comes through very clearly: "If it is possible, as far as it depends on you, live at peace with everyone."

We can't avoid all conflicts. We can't make everyone like us. But from our end, we can live at peace with everyone. That's the great promise implied in these exhortations that form one of the great New Testament Ten Commandments. Difficult people don't have to dominate our lives.

How do we escape them? How do we escape our own difficulties that keep us tangled up with difficult people?

The New Testament presents us with a resource for conflict resolution, a way of disarming difficult people. It's called the peace of Christ. This is actually a powerful weapon that we don't often wield in a practical way.

A contemporary author wrote, "There is no such thing as inner peace. There is only nervousness and death." Jesus told his disciples, "In me you may have peace. In this world you will have trouble. But take heart! I have overcome the world." Christ's peace is something that overcomes the hassles of a world full of difficult people. It's greater than anything the world can give; it transcends human understanding. It can "rule in your hearts," acting as an arbiter within, resolving disputes. In other words, it's the one thing that can actually loosen the grip of a pit bull.

Here's why. Christ's peace is based on his reconciling the whole world to himself when he spread out his arms on the cross. The sacrifice of Jesus creates an incredibly wide welcome into grace. Humanity is redefined. Artificial distinctions disappear. We are all one people from the perspective of Calvary.

Colossians explains that Christ's blood makes peace. Ephesians asserts that the cross reconciles groups that have nurtured hostility for generations: "His purpose was to create in himself one new man out of the two, thus making peace." And Corinthians affirms that, being compelled by the love of Christ, we are given a ministry of reconciliation, regarding "no one from a worldly point of view."

What is the point of view that the cross inspires? It's to look at every human being in terms of her need. Human beings need forgiveness. Human beings need grace. We all have to lay our mistakes, the things we cringe about, at the place where Jesus poured out his life.

Seeing people in terms of their needs—that's a Mustard Seed Secret. It's a life-changing promise.

Catch the tears behind the cool shades.

Spot the pain under the angry outburst.

Sense the fear inside the proud body language.

Find the lonely soul within the rude remarks.

Uncover the deep longing beneath the cutting wit.

See the panic under the iron grip.

Pick out the years of disappointment behind the awkward gesture.

Something amazing happens when we look through people to their needs. It's a powerful perspective that can disarm the difficult people in our lives.

When I was in college, I became very close with five other guys in a Bible study group on campus. It was a new and exciting experience for me. I was able to open up in ways I hadn't before.

But one evening a six-foot-five football player burst into our quiet gathering. He extended his hand in all directions and bellowed out his name. Big Wally, I discovered, was the latest addition to our group. For me the spell was broken; I was sure our meetings would never be the same.

During the weeks that followed, I listened resentfully to Wally's opinions boom across the room. Not only were our personalities poles apart, but his All-American airhead religious views were ones I disdained. This primitive extrovert had ruined our tranquil, reflective atmosphere.

Fortunately, our study leader came up with a new way to open our sharing time. He asked us to pray silently for each group member. We were to think of their needs and claim God's assistance in their lives. I prayed for the person on my right, the person on my left, and then came to Wally, who was sitting across from me. Bowing my head, I tried to pray about the biology test he was facing and the girlfriend who had dumped him.

That simple act of blessing jolted me awake. I just couldn't think of Wally in the same way. He required my help, and I needed his.

I began to see things I admired in this guy. The more we prayed together, the more I came to like Wally, until one evening I found myself jumping on a sofa with him, wildly celebrating an answer to prayer. His raw enthusiasm had become infectious rather than offensive.

Praying about someone else's needs can break an otherwise open-and-shut case of animosity. An enemy can't have needs any more than a suspect can have alibis. As soon as they appear, the label disappears.

Why is Joe so obnoxious when he tries to get coworkers over to his "fabulous condo"? Because he desperately needs friends; he has no one close to give him feedback and develop his social skills.

Why is Sally so annoying when all she wants is for you to baby-sit her kids? Because she's desperately looking for someone to take care of her like her parents never did.

Why does Mike drive everyone nuts complaining about the betrayals of women? Because it's the only way he can release the anger that's about to consume him.

All of us are trying to have our needs met in some way. So many protracted battles would fade if we acknowledged that. We're all weak, sinful human beings in need of grace. So, instead of making every effort to coddle our resentments and rehearse our accusations, we can make every effort to live at peace. We're going to be expending emotional energy anyway; we might as well invest it in something that counts.

Acknowledging that people have needs, however, doesn't mean we have to rescue them. Part of the problem with difficult people is that they want to make us responsible for their misery. Conflicts are based on the premise, "You should be meeting my needs and you're not doing it." Sometimes we fall for that line and get stuck in a relationship with a difficult person.

To disentangle, it helps to understand that everyone has to make his own peace — by taking his needs to Christ. Jesus' peace is the ultimate solution. Nothing else can substitute for that. When Paul was planning a visit to a church in Corinth torn by scandals and lawsuits, he vowed "to know nothing while I was with you except Jesus Christ and him crucified."

Instead of trying to rescue difficult people, we can point them to the place where we all need to go. Everyone needs to start with grace.

Instead of fretting over the way "those people" are, come as *you* are.

Instead of being flabbergasted by failures, be amazed by grace.

Instead of blaming, confess.

Instead of controlling, be captured.

Instead of getting others to carry your burdens, lay them down.

Instead of pointing accusations, lift up empty hands.

Leave that chip on your shoulder with the one shouldering his own cross. We all need to follow him. It's only in the process of

seeking to meet our needs in the peace of Christ that we can begin to help meet each other's needs.

Late one evening, three men conversed in a small flat in Budapest—a Lutheran pastor named Richard, his landlord, and Borila, a huge soldier on leave from the front.* Borila dominated the conversation, boasting of his adventures in ethnic cleansing in the Balkans. He said he'd killed hundreds of Jews in one village with his own hands.

Pastor Richard was not a man who could remain silent about cruelty, so he replied: "It's a frightening story, but I don't fear for the Jews—God will compensate them for what they have suffered. I ask myself with anguish what will happen to the murderers when they stand before God's judgment."

Borila quickly took offense. The landlord, attempting to prevent an ugly scene, told both men that they were guests in his house, and steered the conversation to more pleasant things.

Eventually, it came out that the Jew-killer was also a lover of music. He'd been captivated by Ukrainian folk songs while on duty in that country and longed to hear them again. Richard started to look past this beast of a man to this soft spot within. And he decided to take a chance.

Bringing Borila up to his apartment, he began playing a few Ukrainian melodies on the piano—softly, so as not to awaken his wife and baby son. After a bit the pastor could see the soldier was deeply moved by the music. He stopped playing and said, "If you look through that curtain you can see someone is asleep in the next room. It's my wife, Sabina. Her parents, her sisters, and her twelve-year-old brother were all killed. You told me you killed hundreds of Jews near the town where they were taken. I guess we can assume you are the murderer of her family."

---

* This story is a paraphrase of one recorded by Richard Wurmbrand in *In God's Underground* (New York: Bantam Books, 1977), pp. 229-233.

Borila leaped from his chair, his eyes ablaze, looking as if he could strangle the pastor. But Richard calmed him by proposing an experiment: "I shall wake my wife and tell her who you are and what you have done. I can tell you what will happen. My wife will not speak one word of reproach! She'll embrace you as if you were her brother. She'll bring you supper, the best things she has in the house."

Richard then came to the punch line: "If Sabina, who is a sinner like us all, can forgive and love like this, imagine how Jesus, who is perfect Love, can forgive and love you!" He urged Borila to return to God and seek forgiveness.

The man suddenly melted. Rocking back and forth, he sobbed out his confession: "I'm a murderer; I'm soaked in blood . . ."

Richard guided him to his knees and began praying. Borila, who'd never said a prayer in his life, simply begged for forgiveness over and over.

Then the pastor walked into the bedroom, gently awakened his wife, and told her all that had just happened. She came out in her dressing gown and extended her hands to the huge, tear-stained soldier. He collapsed in her arms and they both wept together. Finally, Sabina went into the kitchen to prepare some food.

Richard thought that his guest could use a further reinforcement of grace, because he only now sensed the horror of his crimes. So he stepped into the next room and returned with his two-year-old son, Mihai, fast asleep in his arms. Borila jumped back in dismay; it had been only hours since he'd boasted of killing Jewish children in their parents' arms. Now this sight seemed an unbearable reproach, and he expected a withering rebuke. Instead, Richard leaned forward and said, "Do you see how quietly he sleeps? You are like a newborn child who can rest in the Father's arms. The blood that Jesus shed has cleansed you."

Looking down at Mihai, Borila felt—for the first time in ages—a surge of hope. After rejoining his regiment, he laid aside his weapons and volunteered to rescue the wounded under fire.

All of us are disarmed when we come to the right place for peace. All of us come away empty-handed and open-hearted.

Cited:

Live in harmony—Romans 12:16
Mutual edification—Romans 14:19
Peace with all—Hebrews 12:14
Peace with each other—1 Thessalonians 5:13
Perfectly united—1 Corinthians 1:10
One as we are one—John 17:21
If possible—Romans 12:18
Overcome the world—John 16:33
Not as the world gives—John 14:27
Transcends understanding—Philippians 4:7
Let peace rule in your hearts—Colossians 3:15;
    Philippians 4:6
Blood makes peace—Colossians 1:20
Hostile groups—Ephesians 2:15
Ministry of reconciliation—2 Corinthians 5:14-19
Know nothing but Christ—1 Corinthians 2:2

CHAPTER TEN

Make A STAND

Resist best by bearing witness against the Enemy

A WOMAN with an SUV full of noisy youngsters was so distracted by their antics behind her that she rolled right through a stop sign. Another driver had to slam on his breaks to avoid a collision. He leaned out his window and yelled, "Lady, don't you know when to stop?"

She glanced at the backseat and replied indignantly, "What makes you think they're all mine?"

Stopping is important. Sometimes we don't really get that message because we're distracted by so many other things. We can misinterpret the basic fact that strategic stops help us avoid crashing. I once met a man who did everything except actually stop.

Jack had struggled long and hard with a sexual addiction and, after years of frustration, finally hit a breakthrough. I wanted him to spell it out for a TV show I was planning. So for two hours I queried and listened to this very bright and articulate man, whose wife and young son were relaxing in their hotel room nearby.

Jack had begun to see his addiction as a mistaken attempt to meet a very legitimate need. He'd realized that, as a sex addict, he needed satisfying relationships with other adults—people unlike his father, who'd been short on love and affection. His desires simply needed to be redirected away from sexuality.

Jack believed temptation had such power over him for so long precisely because it scared him to death. He locked onto it: "This could destroy my family." So, rather than beg God, "Please set me free," he began thanking his Lord that he was free. If he fell into sin, he determined not to let it drag him down but to go on believing that Christ had given him new life.

Some time later I was greatly saddened to learn Jack had to resign as director of a ministry for people struggling with sexual problems. Apparently, he'd engaged in inappropriate behavior with a young counselee at his center.

When I next talked to him, Jack explained. His attempts to provide someone with a healthy, loving relationship had gone too far. He'd begun to rationalize that his demonstrations of affection were part of therapy. But unfortunately, they'd progressed into something sexual.

Looking back, I get the feeling that Jack had grown so tired of staring down sin with fear and loathing that he wanted to see only good. He'd resisted for so long with such a sense of failure that he wanted to stop fighting and simply claim victory. He tried very hard to transform every pull toward the old life into something that could be legitimately fulfilled—in a slightly revised way.

But sometimes we just need to stop. Sometimes we need to resist, to say no. The New Testament emphasizes that point in various ways. It includes self-control in almost every list of essential virtues. It urges us to flee from sinful desires and "avoid every kind of evil." It promises that if we resist this roaring lion, the Devil, he will flee from us. It calls us to "put to death . . . whatever belongs to your earthly nature." Hebrews even asks if we've ever battled sin "to the point of shedding your blood."

Admittedly, we don't want to get stuck in a religion of avoidance. We don't want our lives centered on sin. But sometimes, especially when a mistake starts turning into a habit, we do need to make a decisive about-face.

If we never resist, we'll never confront the Tyranny of Now. Almost all habits are habits because of the dictatorship of this moment. We know all about the benefits of later; we know very well what's best in the long run. It's the benefit of now that gets us. It's always this temporary, forgivable detour that pulls us back into trouble. As psychologist Rodger K. Bufford explained: "Choosing to be thin next week rather than to eat candy next week poses no problem. The difficulty occurs when we must choose between eating candy now and being thin next week." Oscar Wilde put it more simply: "I can resist anything except temptation."

The Tyranny of Now gives us a great alibi: Sorry! Lost my head. Didn't know what I was doing! We often try to make what is premeditated appear spontaneous. We ignore the many times we actually rehearsed our "little sin" in our minds before "tripping" into it.

Yes, sometimes we do have to stand up and fight. All the good qualities the Spirit is building inside us can be neutralized by a failure to draw a line of resistance.

But how do we resist successfully? For most of us, willpower is like whistling in the dark. We're not sure it will bail us out when we call on it, because we're not really sure where we stand—resist or give in? We're like the guy lost in a big city who asked a friend to pick him up, saying, "Well, I'm in a phone booth on the corner of Walk and Don't Walk."

Wouldn't it be great if we could have the confidence of some monks John Chrysostom observed who "wage war on the devil as though they were performing a dance."

Fortunately, the New Testament doesn't just tell us to take two tablets of self-control and call in the morning. It gives us some excellent advice on how best to resist.

The apostle John claimed there is a way to overcome the whole world: "And his commands are not burdensome, for everyone born of God overcomes the world. This is the victory that has overcome the world, even our faith. Who is it that overcomes the world? Only he who believes that Jesus is the Son of God."

We need to resist evil. But it's our faith that overcomes the world. How do we put these two things together? The answer is a great Mustard Seed Secret: We resist best in a way that expresses faith. In other words, our success is determined by expressing positive beliefs about God as we say no to evil.

The book of Revelation echoes the point. It describes those who overcome "the accuser of our brothers," Satan, in this way: "They overcame him by the blood of the Lamb and by the word of their testimony . . ."

How do we get the upper hand over the world, the flesh, and the Devil? By the power of Christ. And by the word of testimony. In other words, by talking back! We're not silent before that Accuser. We don't huddle on the defensive. We are witnesses for the prosecution. We give counter-testimony. We speak boldly for the truth.

We resist best by bearing witness against the enemy. That's a life-changing promise.

I remember one gloomy day as a young man with an old habit, trying to crawl out from under yet another defeat. It had been one of those premeditated, deliberate falls. Everything was blurry; I wanted to acknowledge before God that I had done wrong, but it was hard to say anything that didn't ring hollow.

How do you express repentance meaningfully . . . for the fiftieth time? How do you feel anything? How do you find some handle for the will, some inspiration for resistance?

I tried to pray and lay out my jaded soul before God, asking for help. But my words kept bouncing off the ceiling.

Then I started looking in the Bible for something that might nourish me awake. My eyes fell on Luke's account of Pilate caught between an innocent Jesus and an angry mob. The Roman governor couldn't get an answer to his repeated question, "What crime has this man committed?" The crowd just kept chanting, "Crucify him! Crucify him!" Pilate suggested a halfway measure: How about if we give the Nazarene a good whipping and then let him go? The mob was in no mood for compromise: "But they were insistent and urgent, demanding with loud cries that He should be crucified. And their voices prevailed."

That last sentence fell on me like a gavel. "Their voices prevailed." That was what had just happened to me! Temptation had been urgent, demanding and loud in my head, the chant of the carnal nature. And I knew exactly what it required of me: to deny the lordship of Jesus over this area of my life (temporarily, of course). I had to turn my back on him. Yes, the same ugly shout had prevailed over me too.

For some reason those words electrified my resolve. What I'd found was a personal battle cry. The next time this destructive habit tried to get cozy in the seat beside me, I would hear the echo of a bloodthirsty mob, "Crucify him!" And I would talk back: There's no way I'm going to let those shouts become the last word.

"Their voices prevailed" (a bit like "Remember the Alamo!") — that little phrase helped me overcome a tendency to go limp whenever temptation bullied. It sparked a stand; it fired up a statement of faith: I want to honor the Christ who gave up his life. I want to choose him above the voices of the crowd.

Each of us can find our own personal battle cries in the Bible; we can find truths we want to affirm, truths that expose the lies of our adversary. We resist best by bearing witness. What does this mean in practical terms? When that roaring lion gets in your face, throw the Word at him as fast as you can. That's what Jesus did when Satan ambushed him in a wilderness and fired off his best three shots.

For example, say the enemy comes with his favorite quip: "Do it now."

You shoot back: "I tell you, now is the time of God's favor, now is the day of salvation."

He persists, "Come on. It's no big deal."

You reply, "Who are you kidding? 'Can a man scoop fire into his lap without his clothes being burned?'"

"I suppose it's going to kill you."

"Evil desires wage 'war against the soul.'"

"But think about it, wouldn't it be nice . . ."

"I'll stand with Moses who 'chose to be mistreated along with the people of God rather than to enjoy the pleasures of sin for a short time.'"

"You're all by yourself, fool. No one's going to know. Why be miserable?"

"I rebuke you in Christ's name. I resist 'firm in the faith' knowing that my 'brothers throughout the world are undergoing the same kind of sufferings.'"

The point, of course, is not to get into an extended dialogue. It's to resist with the Word so the Enemy will flee from you. You're affirming the positive values you do believe in. If you can keep doing that for a bit, Scripture itself will rescue you. As the double-edged sword of the Spirit, it can cut through the most belligerent temptations.

Fighting back on your own can't even cut through butter. It's like bragging that your dog can lick anyone. When it comes to temptation, the size of the fight in the dog shrinks pretty quickly. What we need instead is the spunky faith of a youthful David who cried out, "You come against me with sword and spear and javelin, but I come against you in the name of the LORD Almighty, the God of the armies of Israel, whom you have defied."

It's good to know that El Shaddai goes into battle on our behalf, "a victorious warrior" who snatches us from the jaws of the tyrant

and who "will exult over you with joy." But above all, it's good to know that Christ's love can find us wherever we are and help us make a stand when we feel overwhelmed.

I'll never forget the time he had to rescue me—by the scruff of my neck. It happened when my marriage was dissolving and I was feeling terribly empty and vulnerable. I started lying awake at night thinking about a certain client who represented the answer to all my dreams.

The problem had started out very slowly in the woman's taste-fully decorated office with tall cypress trees waving outside. Something was beckoning me. This woman always seemed to have writing projects that paid well and challenged me creatively. We had a lot to talk about. And we kept talking. Pretty soon we were con-versing about her childhood, her teenagers, her frustrations with a dead church, her hopes for the future.

And I was slipping. I was slipping because she appeared to be the most beautiful, the most spiritual, the most fascinating creature on earth. At first I tried to tell myself this was just a good Christian friendship. But then I started obsessing about her, imagining her as the one individual who could truly fulfill me.

I had to do something. Even though this client and I hadn't done anything outwardly inappropriate, in my own mind an affair began to seem the most natural thing in the world. So late at night, lying alone, I agonized about how to end the relationship. This client was a good source of income. But I couldn't continue work-ing with her. Should I just stop? She'd keep calling. Should I tell her how I felt? Who knew where that might lead.

Most of all, I was looking for a way to stop my own emotions. Around midnight I began reading the words of Jesus. I needed to hear his voice above my own conflicted thoughts. I plowed aimlessly through the gospel of Matthew until one statement hit me between the eyes: "Whoever finds his life will lose it, and whoever loses his life for my sake will find it." That text immediately brought to mind a verse from James: "Every good and perfect gift is from above, coming down from the Father of the heavenly lights."

Yes, here was something to grab hold of. I'd been agonizing because I believed this woman was my last hope for intimacy. I didn't want to die without experiencing that, without anyone ever really knowing me. It was hard to give that up.

But what I needed was to give it up for Christ's sake. If I grabbed for immediate emotional intimacy, trying to make it happen on my own, then it would surely slip through my fingers. But if I refused to follow my fantasies and to seek intimacy outside of his will, then I would find what I was looking for.

At that very moment, Jesus' words became as real to me as the law of gravity. Their truth sank into my bones. Yes, every perfect gift, every gift worth having, is his alone to give. Intimacy will happen within a commitment to live by faith. Nothing of value will come to me outside of God's will.

So—without reservation—I made a choice. I would say goodbye to my client clearly, no strings attached. But I'd do so discreetly, no gushing. In the dead of that night, I chose God altogether—expressing it in a voice that sounded weak and hoarse. But I will never forget the surge of love that swept through me right then. I was lying there with nothing but the Word to fend off the emotional storm raging around me. Yet I felt confident and at peace. I don't think I've ever felt closer to Christ. I wanted to swear an undying allegiance to the One who speaks so truly and absolutely, the One who enables us to walk in the Way of Love.

Cited:

Self-control—2 Peter 1:6; 1 Peter 1:13; 4:7; 5:8; 1
    Thessalonians 5:6,8; 1 Timothy 3:2
Flee from—2 Timothy 2:22

Avoid every kind of evil—1 Thessalonians 5:22
Resist the lion—James 4:7; 1 Peter 5:9
Put to death—Colossians 3:5
Shedding your blood—Hebrews 12:4
Overcome the world—1 John 5:3-5
Word of testimony—Revelation 12:10-11
Their voices prevailed—Luke 23:20-23, AMP
Day of salvation—2 Corinthians 6:2
Fire into lap—Proverbs 6:27
War against the soul—1 Peter 2:11
Short pleasures—Hebrews 11:25
Same sufferings—1 Peter 5:9
David's battle cry—1 Samuel 17:45
Warrior God—Psalms 24:7-8; 45:3-4; 74:14; Zephaniah
    3:17, NASB
Find and lose—Matthew 10:39
Good and perfect gift—James 1:17
Power in the inner man—Ephesians 3:16

 **EXPRESSED**

SHORTLY AFTER World War II, the bombed-out city of Naples was filled with bands of young orphans and outcasts called *scugnizzi*.* They lived on the streets, begging, pilfering, and sometimes assisting older criminals. These kids were tough, wily, and apparently unreachable. But twenty-five-year-old Father Mario Borrelli wanted to try. He felt compelled to love in the way Christ had loved. So, each night after his regular duties, he became a *scugnizzi*.

Dressed in a ragged and filthy get-up, he started begging at the Naples railroad terminal. The other young toughs were impressed by his style: just the right mixture of humor and pathetic humility. When a gang leader swaggered up and demanded half his take, Mario beat him up. That really impressed the guys.

This incognito priest slept on basement gratings covered with old newspapers, just like the others. Soon he was getting to know his new companions well as they talked around fires, heating up their

---

* This story is a paraphrase of one recorded by Frederic Sondern Jr. in "Don Vesovio and the House of the Urchin," *Reader's Digest Teenage Treasure, vol. 3* (Pleasantville, NY: Reader's Digest Association, 1957), pp. 28-32.

scraps of food in old tin cans. He had something to express about the God who took on human flesh. And Mario discovered that all of them, even the most bitter and hardened, had a longing for home, affection, and security.

After winter arrived, Mario informed the gang that he'd found a place for them to stay, the abandoned ruins of the church of Saint Gennaro. Slowly he transformed the structure into a home and started providing the boys with nourishing meals.

One night Mario appeared in full clerical robes. After his buddies stopped laughing, he explained that he was, in fact, a priest. By this time the bonds he'd established were strong enough to make them stay; Mario had won their respect. And so the House of the Urchin was established, where young throwaways could find a home, hope, and the streetwise spiritual guidance of Mario Borrelli.

Wonderful things happen when we take a step after the Christ who invaded this planet with his love. Jesus made a big splash in the human neighborhood, and he invites us to splash along with him. That's really the Secret of the Mustard Seed. So much good is unleashed when we respond to that greatest of all principles, that life-changing promise: "Love one another as I have loved you." A new creation tumbles out when we express something of how we have been loved, how we have been forgiven, how we have been chosen and justified and healed and built up. Jesus is made flesh again.

Think about the things that happened when he appeared on a seashore, or walked down a street, or came into a room.

A twelve-year-old child lying cold and pale amid the wail of mourners might suddenly open her eyes and ask Mom for breakfast.

A roaring sea, sending wave after wave over a tiny fishing boat, might suddenly quiet into a glassy lake.

A man who's been lying in a paralyzed heap for thirty-eight years might find one day he can walk—and skip and jump like a schoolboy.

A terribly disfigured leper might one day find his skin as smooth as a baby's.

Jesus' presence shakes things up. Life suddenly becomes open-ended, filled with possibilities. That's God's signature through the whole Bible. Following him, you're never stuck between a rock and a hard place. The rock just might erupt into a spring of water. You're never up against the wall. A wall as hefty as Jericho's might just crumble before shouts of praise.

Things aren't always what they seem. God's often got something else up his sleeve. Before you know it, water turns into wine. Cripples turn into acrobats. Bleached bones assemble into a living army. The king of cruel Assyria becomes a humble penitent. The cross, an instrument of torture, is manhandled into a means of salvation.

God turns nature itself upside down and inside out. He turns day into night for stubborn Pharaoh. He turns night into day for shepherds watching their flocks near Bethlehem. He makes a fig tree wither for the disciples and dead wood blossom for Aaron.

That's who is still making a splash here. That's the reality we have to absorb if we're going to experience the Secret of the Mustard Seed. If we limit God, if we keep him in a corner of our lives, if we view him only as a deity in the distance, then we won't see this seed grow into a glorious tree spreading its fruit against the big sky.

There's a lot of this and that in our lives. We have so many options these days, so many alternatives to check out. And that can be a good thing. But sometimes it's like we've got one hand on the diet book and the other in the cookie jar. When it comes to love, we need to settle it; we need to make a commitment. Love is a decision to give ourselves away to the right person. It isn't a decision to visit him once a week, like we might a relative in a nursing home. It isn't a decision to use him as an accessory in our lives, like a certain outfit that helps us look our best. It isn't a decision to serve him and something else. When we divide our allegiance, we dilute our faith.

It's time to respond in kind to the love God has lavished on us. It's time to invest ourselves in his life-changing promises. We have plenty of evidence that they can work dramatically in human life. Now we need to give them room, to reach higher, and deeper, and wider.

And what will help us make our commitment real is to give it a voice. Love is something that needs to be expressed. Sometimes you hear married people claim that they really do love their spouse, they just aren't very good at expressing it. But that's hard to buy. Not good at it? No one is asking you to write sonnets. Just fix him a special meal—cheerfully. Or take her to a classy restaurant—unexpectedly.

Love unexpressed doesn't exist. It's an illusion. It's like saying, I'm really a pianist but I just don't know how to work the keys.

Love can only grow as it's given a voice. It's time to express our love for the one-and-only God, to affirm our allegiance to the Almighty, the Lord of lords, the Creator and Redeemer, to voice our trust in the one whose thoughts are as high above ours as the heavens are above the earth, to fix our gaze on the One who calls us to have no other gods before him.

Mark Twain's wife detested her famous husband's habit of swearing and tried many times to reform the man's tongue. One day the writer cut himself while shaving and blew through his entire store of expletives. When he'd finished, his wife steadily repeated every phrase. Twain turned from the mirror and replied, "You have the words, dear, but you don't know the tune."

When it comes to expressing love for God, we often recite the words without really getting the tune. What we need is the moral equivalent of hammering our thumbs. We need to find something we truly admire about Christ that will inspire us to take a Mustard Seed step after him. That's how we find our voices. That's how we lift up our lives as a living sacrifice. That's how we can express love with all the gusto of a sailor spewing epithets.

It's time to respond in kind to the God of infinite possibilities. It's time to begin our own Mustard Seed adventure.

∞

Lord, enable me to express love more surely, more eloquently, more powerfully.

I want to express love by extending my faith on tiptoe, throwing it out there farther. Yes, it's possible to stretch until God makes more of me, spreading my branches toward the big sky. Yes, I want to focus more intently on the One who writes my name on his palm and numbers the hairs on my head.

I want to express love by overflowing with thanks, alive to more providences, perceiving more blessings in disguise. Yes, it's possible to lift up a cascade of leaves toward the God who creates with light and feel the sap of his Spirit make my world green.

I want to express love by listening with the ear of a disciple. Keep me reaching out for more, exploring new territory. Yes, it's possible to sink my roots deep into the inexhaustible supply of his truth.

I want to express love by forgiving for good, by applying those thick, red brush strokes where I've only watercolored before. Yes, it's possible to heal old wounds with Christ's pardon blossoming brightly around me.

I want to express love by praising with all my heart and soul. I want to sing the God uncontainable, flowering in the grass, sparkling in the heavens, healing human hearts. Yes, it's possible to give him glorious weight, give him leverage, and watch him lift every bit of baggage from my shoulders.

I want to express love by practicing the musical language of grace. Yes, it's possible to turn on a light in someone's eyes, to place a song in someone's heart. It's possible to become a great spreading tree, giving the birds of the air good shelter.

I want to express love by persisting more patiently. Yes, it's possible to run inspired, with my feet barely grazing the ground, with my eyes fixed on the Christ who still dazzles with his magical touch.

I want to express love by opening my hand and my heart. Yes, it's possible to find a good life by giving it away.

I want to express love by spreading the peace of Christ and the riches of reconciliation. Yes, it's possible to disarm the most difficult people around me by spotlighting their needs instead of my annoyances.

And finally, I want to express love by standing firm, immovable. Yes, it's possible to resist with confidence, bearing witness instead of shaking in my boots, swearing allegiance by yards, instead of yielding by inches.

∽

These are the qualities most worth fleshing out; these are the skills that echo eternally. They form the Way of Love, the winsome virtues worth their weight in Van Gogh's colors or Mozart's notes. The quality of our lives is determined by how much we invest in them, how much we express.

Goodness doesn't have to be confined to the conventional or the colorless. It can become a glorious endeavor that adds our own individual brush strokes to the great canvas of those who are "transformed into his likeness with ever-increasing glory." Yes, I believe we can lighten the whole world with these Secrets of the Mustard Seed.

About THE AUTHOR

STEVEN MOSLEY has been making the Bible come alive for contemporary audiences all over the world since 1984 as an award-winning scriptwriter and producer for Christian television. His telecast series include *Soul Care, Jesus Face to Face,* and *Truths That Change Us Inside.* He also conducts "Wield the Word" weekend seminars around the United States, featuring a dramatic presentation: "Chosen Garment—The Whole Bible in One Act." Steven is the author of ten books, including *Glimpses of God* and *Burned Out on Being Good.* He lives in Huntington Beach, California, with his wife, Marilyn.

THOUGHTFUL BOOKS FOR FURTHERING YOUR FAITH.

Love Walked Among Us

Maybe you know who Jesus is—but do you know what he was like as a person? Discover the personal side of Jesus.
(Paul Miller)

Love Your God with All Your Mind

Have you really thought about your faith? This book examines the role of reason in faith, helping you use your intellect to further God's kingdom.
(J.P. Moreland)

To get your copies, visit your local bookstore, call 1-800-366-7788, or log on to www.navpress.com. Ask for a FREE catalog of NavPress products. Offer #BPA.